Soldiers and Armies

Also by Ernest E. Tucker

The Story of Fighting Ships

The Story of Knights and Armor

Soldiers and Armies:
Men at War Through the Ages

BY ERNEST E. TUCKER

Illustrated by W. T. Mars

Lothrop, Lee & Shepard Co., Inc.

NEW YORK

To My Father, Irwin St. John Tucker

Contents

INTRODUCTION
What Is a Soldier?

Ask a child, "What is a soldier?" and the chances are he will answer, "A soldier is a man who fights." This is a sensible enough answer, but it is not really precise. If you accept the child's definition, a heavyweight champion is a soldier; so were the Western sheriffs and badmen of legend; so was Robin Hood, battling the sheriff's men in Sherwood Forest. But we mean none of these when we think of a soldier.

The dictionary definition is, "A man engaged in military services; one whose profession is military." The second part of this definition, if taken literally, would exclude all the millions of men over the centuries who were tailors or mechanics or schoolteachers, yet who found themselves spending at least part of their lives in an army. They were soldiers, but it wasn't their profession.

The first part of the definition, "A man engaged in military services," is accurate enough but it's too pale, somehow. It doesn't *sound* like a soldier—a word which makes many people think of the rattle of drums and the sound of trumpets, of waving flags and marching feet.

War isn't like that, of course. Trumpets and flags are only a very small part of it. War is hardship, and boredom, and fear; it's being sent places you don't want to go and told to do things you don't want to do. Most people hate and fear war, and yet they usually—nowadays, at least—honor and respect the men who fight it: the soldiers.

"Soldier" is a very old word. The dictionary traces it back through various spellings to the Roman camp slang word *solidarius,* meaning a man who was paid with a *solidus,* a piece of money. Originally solidus meant just what "solid" means today.

"Soldier" can signify a GI Joe in olive-drab battle dress, or a Roman legionary with a square shield and an 8-foot spear, or a Frenchman in a white satin coat and cocked hat. A soldier may be one of an army numbering in the millions or one of a corporal's guard. He may labor under the inhuman discipline of a Frederick the Great, or be as casually organized as an American rifleman of the Revolution. He may be a Napoleon or a fumble-fingered private; he may fight with a bronze sword or by pushing buttons in an underground control point.

Soldiers can battle for a noble purpose like freedom, or for an ignoble one like conquest or loot. A soldier can die heroically in an unjust cause, as thousands of Germans did for Adolf Hitler; or he can be a coward in a noble cause, like some American militiamen of the Revolution who sneaked home when battle was imminent.

Some things soldiers seem always to have shared. A few have enjoyed the drama, danger, and excitement of warfare, but most have disliked it intensely and longed for home. In spite of the fact that millions of men have borne arms throughout history, there are very scanty records of private soldiers. Almost without exception the soldiers who did keep diaries seem to have been pre-occupied with getting enough to eat, keeping warm, and finding a comfortable place to sleep. Most ex-soldiers will confirm the impressions of those who have left records: that war, in general, consists of long periods of acute boredom punctuated by moments of acute terror.

Sometimes soldiers have been respected and feared, as were the samurai, the warrior caste of Japan. Some-times they have been respected and admired, as were the phalangites of ancient Sparta and as our soldiers are today. Sometimes they were despised as following a low and undignified calling, as in ancient China; or bitterly hated, as were the "free companies" which roamed Europe in the late Middle Ages.

Oddly enough, at a time when soldiers were considered to be hardly more than animals—some two hundred years ago—war was regarded as just another form of politics, nothing to be very frightened of, nothing to work very hard at averting. Now, when the word "war" connotes the ultimate in horror, "soldier" means brother Joe or the nice guy next door.

This book is intended to give a glimpse of soldiers throughout the ages. It is necessarily very incomplete. Any comprehensive examination of soldiers, in every age and in every country, would require a good-sized library. The book will tell you about soldiers in some of the most important times of world history; how they fought, how their armies were organized, and how the civilians of their times looked upon them.

The individual soldiers in the book, like Gaius Lucius
Dervigilius or Private Harry Jenkins, are, of course,
imaginary. At least they are imaginary in the sense that
these particular men never really lived. But there were
many actual soldiers in those periods who did live, talk,
and think as Gaius, Harry, and the other soldiers in this
book do.

CHAPTER I

Primitive Warriors

One day in the season when the leaves turn red, a young hunter came running up to White Stone Caves. He reported breathlessly that there were other people in the valley, near Where the River Bends.

Kills Buffalo, the chief of the little tribe of cave dwellers, was interested, but neither surprised nor alarmed. Everyone knew that there were other people who lived outside the broad valley. From time to time these others entered the valley, but nobody bothered them. Why should they?

But the young hunter had more disturbing news. These other people had shouted at him in a strange tongue and made threatening gestures, and one had thrown a spear. Kills Buffalo grunted in astonishment; he had never heard of anyone acting like that. He thought about it for three days, a slow and tiring process for him, and in the end he decided simply to go and see for himself.

He came back from his mission in a terrible rage. It was as the young hunter said. There were strange people who had built brush huts near Where the River Bends.

Kills Buffalo began telling the tribe about it, eking out their crude spoken language in pantomime, as hunters did when they recounted the killing of a boar. His words took on a chanting rhythm, and his movements became a sort of dance.

The tribe began to sway in unison as they listened. Kills Buffalo told them that the strangers were catching

the tribe's fish. No one had ever thought of the fish as belonging to the tribe, but now that Kills Buffalo said it, they realized it must be so. The chief, working himself up to a frenzy, told how the strangers had discovered him and chased him, throwing stones and flint-headed spears.

His frenzy communicated itself to the others. The men —all males over fourteen up to the tribe's elders, who were about forty—joined the chief in his dance. Although they did not know it, they were doing a war dance, working themselves into a fighting pitch by howling threats and going through the motions of fighting. Finally they dashed off, waving their clubs and spears, to drive the now-hated strangers out of their valley.

The battle was short and fierce. Kills Buffalo remembered it as if in a dream—swinging his stone-headed hatchet at the strangers, being hit with a club, howling and whooping as he and the tribe chased the intruders. Much later he found himself alone in the trees. It was nearly dark and his blood lust had vanished. He shivered when he heard animals prowling in the forest. Later he would retell at great length, and with great pride, his exploits in expelling the intruders. But just now he was lonely and frightened, and a little bewildered by the whole thing.

So soldiers usually feel after a battle. But was this primitive man, who drove the unwelcome strangers away, a soldier?

No, he was not. A fighting man, a warrior, perhaps; but to merit the title of soldier something more is needed. Kills Buffalo went to "war" in the same spirit that he would have joined with his fellows in hunting a wild boar or chasing away an inquisitive bear. They were not warlike, those long dead ancestors of ours. The popular idea of a cave man as a ferocious, aggressive character, forever battling with other cave men, finds little favor with modern anthropologists.

Kills Buffalo probably did not think of war as being something different from any other kind of activity. Not until many thousands of years after he was dead and forgotten would men set out deliberately to make war. And even then, they did not think of soldiers as being set apart from the rest of the adult males of the group.

In *Warfare,* an excellent book on military methods by several experts in the field, Brigadier General Oliver L. Spaulding, U.S.A., says: "Government [that is, primitive government] was merely an association of individuals, generally more or less related by blood, for mutual aid. . . . The relations of the government to the army were simple, for the two were identical—the whole body of the tribe, physically and mentally qualified, considered from the alternative points of view of peace and war. The primitive elements of warfare seem to be two only—surprise, and individual strength and skill."

At this stage in human history warfare consisted of ambushes and raids, in which every able-bodied man of the tribe took part. It wasn't a case of a tribe being at peace, then shifting into a state of war. There were raids whenever the opportunity presented itself, or whenever the young bloods of the tribe felt the need for a little excitement. At first the raids were prompted, most likely, by a simple desire for plunder—furs, perhaps, or food, or even slaves. There was no question of right or wrong involved. It was simply, "Those other people have something we want. Let's go take it."

Very early another element was mixed in: the element of fighting for the sake of personal prestige. Among the American Indians, the Pawnee warrior ran off with the Wichita ponies, not because he needed more ponies but because their possession marked him as an outstanding warrior. The bigger the pony herd he owned, the better

warrior he was. The Cheyenne brave "counted coup"—
touched a slain or wounded foe—for no other reason than
that the act proved his bravery. An enemy scalp was a
trophy; the man who took it was so contemptuous of his
foes that he lingered in a place of danger to get it.

Many books have been written about the fighting customs of primitive peoples. Sometimes they seem to have
fought for no reason at all, or at least for no reason that
we can understand. The modern slang term "just for
kicks" perhaps comes as close as anything to describing
it. Among the Maoris, for instance, the Polynesian people
who live in New Zealand, it was customary to have battles arranged ahead of time, for all the world like a football game. When the two sides met, if they found that
one side was inferior in numbers, their enemies would
lend them enough men to make everything equal! And
the borrowed warriors fought as ardently as the rest.

The North American Indians were formidable fighters. Poorly organized, comparatively few in number,
with weapons far inferior, they fought bitterly against
the crushing tide of the white man's advance. There is
nothing to indicate that the individual white man was
any braver or any better fighter than the individual
Iroquois or Sioux.

Like the Maoris, the Zulus, and the Sudanese, the
American Indians were excellent warriors. But they were
not soldiers. What was missing in primitive governments,
such as General Spaulding was writing about, was discipline and organization.

A primitive tribe could make a sudden raid for plunder
or ambush a party of enemies. The raids might be well
planned. The tribesmen often fought bravely, even hero-

ically. But they did not have the discipline, or the organization, or the stamina, to carry out long, complicated campaigns.

For centuries, men of more advanced civilizations have been fighting primitive warriors. From Alexander the Great down to modern times, they report much the same thing: The warriors may be magnificent fighters, as individuals, but as a group they are not so effective. They do not understand cooperation. They are far more formidable when they are attacking than when they are being attacked. They are subject to sudden, unreasoning panic, and may flee just when victory is imminent. Rarely can they carry out that most difficult of military maneuvers, an orderly retreat under attack. They have neither the patience nor the foresight for long-range operations; if they cannot win in short order, they get discouraged and go home. They can be diverted from the object of their attack by the prospect of loot. They are almost impossible to control; they will obey their chiefs or leaders when it suits them, but follow their own whims if they disagree with the chief's orders.

Such criticisms should not be confined to primitive tribes. Much the same charges have been leveled against soldiers of so-called civilized nations. Military history is full of stories of armies falling prey to irrational panic, or throwing away all discipline and reverting to savagery.

But there are many more stories of armies maintaining order and saving themselves under conditions which would have caused a barbarian army to collapse and dissolve. The difference is that sense of cohesion, that willingness to obey orders, which organization and discipline bring.

CHAPTER 2

The First Soldiers

About six thousand years ago, loosely organized tribes in the Middle East and the Orient started to knit themselves together into city-states, under strong rulers who were really little kings. To enforce their authority, and to protect themselves, these early kings gathered around themselves groups of armed men who were the first real soldiers, and the nucleus of the world's first real armies.

These bodyguards were recruited from men who were specialists in fighting, as other men were specialists in herding sheep or tanning leather. With their specialty they began to acquire a professionalism which included, besides skill with weapons, the beginnings of a science of tactics and even strategy. Strategy is the planning done before an army meets the enemy; tactics, the planning done after the armies are in contact.

They also started to develop those qualities which we associate with the word "soldierly": physical courage, esprit de corps, a sense of unity and discipline. Undoubtedly they also began to develop that arrogance and narrow outlook which are unfortunately so often a part of the military mind.

With the employment of professional soldiers the kings embarked on bigger military projects. At first these were probably just the old raids and ambushes on a somewhat larger scale. But the tighter organization of the city-states, which were really small countries, permitted the kings to make more ambitious plans. Real wars, to serve the political purposes of the city-states, began to be fought.

The bodyguards became small standing armies, whose loyalty was to the king; the idea of loyalty to a country had not yet evolved. When a war was imminent the army was enlarged by pressing into service the rest of the able-bodied men of the community. The professionals served then either as a sort of officer corps or as a body of elite troops who bore the brunt of the fighting. The nonprofessional soldiers accepted this scheme readily; they were still not far removed from the old tribal days, when to be a man meant to be a warrior.

Imagine that you are standing on a low hill in ancient Mesopotamia overlooking a vast flat plain. You are in quite modern times, as history goes; it is about four thousand years before the birth of Christ.

Far off to the west are the mud walls and buildings of a city called Amu-Resh—a large city by the standards of those days, a small town by ours. Beyond the city gleam the waters of the broad Euphrates River, and around the mud walls stretch cultivated fields. Most of the landscape, though, is barren and dusty, with patches of thorn bushes, coarse grass, and small shrubs.

It is terribly hot. Great drifts of yellowish dust hang in the air like veils. The dust is being stirred up by thousands of men, divided into two armies, who are moving around on the plain opposite each other. They are real armies, and they are getting ready to fight a real battle. Man has come a long way in terms of military organization since the days of Kills Buffalo and his tribesmen.

Dimly you can hear the thump of drums and tambourines, the droning of ram's horn trumpets, and the chanting of priests. The holy men are behind the two armies, conducting sacrifices which send waves of smoke billowing into the cloudless sky.

One of the stocky men down there in the defending army is named Gilgal the Herdsman. Like his fellows, Gilgal is wearing sandals, a knee-length kilt, and a leather cap. He carries an oblong shield made of wickerwork covered with leather, slung by a strap over his shoulder and provided with arm loops as well. In his belt is stuck a bronze knife ten inches long. His main weapon is a bronze-headed spear, eight feet in length.

The spear, the knife, the shield, are true weapons—that is, they are not tools of hunting or of a trade, pressed into emergency service. In this, too, the army of Amu-Resh shows a great advance over the spur-of-the-moment weapons of Kills Buffalo.

Gilgal's throat is dry and his pulse is jumping. He is frightened to death of being killed or wounded, but he is even more frightened of showing it, so he laughs and jokes with the man next to him.

Looking around at his comrades is a comfort. They appear tough and competent, and their spear points gleam brightly. How can any foe defeat such a fine army? The thought cheers Gilgal. But then in the next minute he is recalling tales of the enemy, who live in a town fifty miles away, a town much like Amu-Resh—how fierce they are, how ruthless, how full of guile. Then he wonders how his little army can hope to defeat such warriors.

Gilgal has the feeling of being just one of a multitude and he enjoys the feeling, but at the same time it seems to him that he is more alone than he ever has been before. With part of his mind he is looking forward to the battle, and with another part he is dreading it and wishing it were over.

Soldiers have always been like that. The Roman plebeian, on his way to fight Hannibal 3,700 years after Gilgal marched out of Amu-Resh, felt the same way. So did the Frankish axeman defending his town against the Vikings, a thousand years later; and the grenadier sweating up Bunker Hill a thousand years after that; and Private Bill Johnson of today.

Members of the king's bodyguard are getting the army of Amu-Resh ready to receive the expected attack. Deploying into formation is a confused, tedious job. The whole idea of armies and wars is new. There is no codified system of commands, issued by the general of the army and passed down through the ranks, until each squad commander sees to it that his men execute them. Even if there had been such commands, Gilgal and his comrades haven't drilled enough to be able to execute them. Getting even this small army, about 3,000 men, into battle formation is a formidable task. The professional soldiers stride up and down the ranks, pushing, hauling, yelling and cursing, trying to line their men up, straighten the ranks, and close the gaps.

The army is drawn up into three lines of battle. The first line is six ranks deep; the second, a few yards to the rear, is four ranks deep; and the reserve line of four

ranks stands about 200 yards to the rear. These reserves
are mostly older men, who will move into action when
they are needed.

The invading army, about a mile away, is drawn up in
a similar formation. Now it begins to move slowly forward, while the drums and horns reach a new pitch of
frenzy.

Between and beside both armies run and dart skirmishers, slingers and bowmen. These are speedy men,
mostly youths, whose job is twofold: to try and get close
enough to the enemy's main body to pick some off, and
to keep the enemy skirmishers away from their own
spearmen. As they dart in and out they keep up a shrill,
staccato yipping. Their light arrows apparently have no
effect on the mass of spearmen. But now and then a
skirmisher falls.

Gilgal's army has finally been shoved and hauled into
position. The king of Amu-Resh, who has some idea of
tactics, has chosen a fairly good spot. One flank of his
army is anchored against a patch of soft sand, and the
other flank is next to an area of big scattered boulders
which will break up the enemy's formation should he try
to march that way.

It becomes harder to see through the clouds of dust.

The soldiers are beginning to shout, a deep-throated
roar which contrasts with the high-pitched yelping of the
skirmishers. The latter are scrambling out of the way
now; they don't want to be caught between the lines.

The army of Amu-Resh is ready to receive the attack.
Their oblong shields are close together. Over them appear the swarthy faces of the soldiers. The bronze spearheads of the first rank project about five feet beyond the

shields. The second rank is just behind the first and their spears stick out perhaps two feet.

The armies are very close to each other now.

The two front ranks come together with an indescribable noise—a dull, grinding, jarring thud. A few shrieks of pain cut through the air.

Then, for a long time, nothing seems to happen. The tight-packed mass of men on the plain is almost motionless. The lines slowly ripple and surge, giving evidence of the tremendous strain they are under. A heaving movement travels from one end to the other, and back. The second line of four ranks moves forward and merges with the first line, adding its weight to the press, and the reserves move up closer.

A man reels out of the melee, staggers aimlessly a few steps, and falls. Another rolls out from under the trampling feet, pulls himself to his hands and knees, and crawls slowly off. Around the flanks hover the skirmishers, watching for targets. Tiny glints of light flash in the air as the sun reflects from arrowheads.

The battle has resolved itself into a swaying, grim shoving-match. The first side to give way will lose. The soldiers have all but forgotten their spears—there is no room to use them. Those behind have set their shields against the backs of the men in front of them and are pushing as hard as they can—as the men behind them are pushing. The reserves on both sides have taken their places and are shoving too.

It is strangely silent. Men pant and sob for breath. Air is precious and there is none to waste on battle cries. In the front ranks, where shield butts against enemy shield, the pressure is incredible. It is impossible to raise an arm,

to thrust with a spear, even to pull a knife from a belt.
If a man loses his footing he cannot fall, but he may sink
down and be crushed or suffocated. Ribs crack, arms and
shoulders are wrenched and sprained. Most of the spears
are wedged uselessly between two men or trapped in a
wicker shield.

The terrible jam goes on for what seems like hours to
the men in the ranks but is actually only about forty
minutes. Then there is the slightest beginning of movement again, a tiny ripple that starts at one end of the
line and surges to the other.

The invaders have moved back a half step.

Gilgal's people sense it and shove harder. The enemy is pushed back another step, then another. A few men shred away from the rear ranks of the invading army and skulk off or run away.

The ripple goes through the lines again. There is a definite surge forward by Gilgal's army as the enemy is pushed back another step, then another.

This is a crucial moment in the battle. If the invaders can pull back swiftly enough, break off the shoving-match, and reform their lines, they will still have a chance to win. But if they give way, or if they turn their backs —as soon as there is room enough to turn—they are doomed. Behind their army the invaders' priests redouble their shouting and drumming. They know the crisis is at hand. Each step backward is a step which cannot be recovered.

The forward thrust of Gilgal's army is beginning to gather a little momentum. The invaders' front ranks are as stubborn as ever but the lessening of pressure from behind puts them at a disadvantage. The rear ranks are giving way. Those who turn and flee, trying to save themselves, are joined by more.

Suddenly the lines of the invaders collapse. Most of their men are running, throwing down spear and shield, intent only on escape. Those still fighting are borne backward by the weight of Gilgal's army. With the lessened pressure, the spears again begin to thrust and probe.

Many of Gilgal's comrades fall, exhausted, sobbing for breath. Those behind, who haven't been under quite such fearful pressure, spring over them yelling and begin the chase.

The battle is over. The invaders are no longer an army but a disorganized, panic-stricken mob, running blindly over the desert. Gilgal and his fellows follow, shouting like fiends.

Amu-Resh is safe from invasion—for a time.

Marching back to the city after the battle, Gilgal began to think that it hadn't been so bad, after all. He remembered the thumping drums and the blaring trumpets, and forgot the hot, thirsty march over the desert. He remembered his excitement and forgot the fright. He remembered the enemy running away and forgot the dreadful crush.

With the strain and pressure gone, Gilgal and his comrades laughed and joked. They did not realize that the laughter was a little too loud, the jokes not very funny. They were vaguely conscious that a vast weight had been lifted from them—the weight of fear. The reaction made them a little lightheaded.

The professional soldiers marched along stolidly, discussing in calm tones various technical aspects of the battle. They felt relieved, too, but they weren't going to show it before all these amateurs.

As they came close to the yellow mud walls of Amu-Resh, the army was greeted by crowds of women and children, who ran out waving palm branches and shouting in triumph. This was a proud moment for Gilgal. He swaggered as he walked and tried to convey the impression that fighting battles was second nature to him, nothing to make a fuss about.

Soldiers have always been like that, too.

Those armies of very ancient times were organized simply enough. They had no cavalry and no chariots; horses and donkeys were not yet in common use as domestic animals. They had no supply corps; every man took what he needed with him, and if he ran short he had to forage for himself. They had no engineers, no doctors —except perhaps some priests with a crude knowledge of medicine—and no well-defined ranks of officers or noncoms. Perhaps the soldiers furnished their own weapons. More likely the king, wary of possible revolt, doled out spears and shields from an armory, and collected them again when the "war" was over.

The strategy and tactics of such an army were crude. Their strategy was probably limited to common-sense rules: Don't start a war against someone three times stronger than you are; meet the enemy far enough away from home so your crops won't be burned; don't leave yourself unguarded against a potential enemy. The professional soldiers were no doubt familiar with elementary tactical precepts: Don't get caught asleep; don't split your force if you can help it; try for surprise if you can; hit the enemy where he is weakest.

These ancient soldiers probably had an intelligence service, scouts and spies. They must have had messengers too, and some way of signaling at a distance, perhaps with smoke.

And of course they had weapons, well enough designed so that the pattern was fixed for thousands of years.

There are three basic kinds of weapons: the kind you swing, the kind you thrust, and the kind you throw. Nowadays weapons that are thrown—missiles—have all but eliminated the other varieties. This class of weapons today includes everything from a rifle bullet on through all the ghastly varieties of ballistic missiles with hydrogen warheads.

The first weapon probably was one of the swinging kind, a club. This developed through various stages to the battle-axe, the mace, and the cutting sword. The first basic thrusting weapon was the spear, originally designed for hunting. Missile weapons in primitive times ranged from thrown stones through varieties of slings to javelins and arrows.

The early axes, swords, and spears were made out of bronze, which isn't as good for the purpose as steel or even iron, but is still quite serviceable. Bronze is a compound made mostly of copper, a common metal, with some of the comparatively rare metal tin added for hardness. It is more brittle than steel and far less resilient.

Bronze swords don't keep a sharp edge and they have to be much thicker in proportion to their length and width than steel swords. But bronze makes good spearheads—one reason why the basic weapon of early armies was the spear.

Facing a single enemy armed with a spear, a man is in no great danger; he can evade the thrust or get inside it and catch hold of the shaft. Facing a thousand enemies armed with spears is something entirely different. Then a man is up against a sort of human porcupine. If he evades one weapon he's likely to spit himself on another. Or if he grabs the shaft of one spear he risks being punctured by the next one.

This kind of fighting demands that the spear wielders stand together, shoulder to shoulder, and act together as a unit. A unit of disciplined spearmen makes a formidable fighting group, but the same number of spearmen, all following their own ideas, would result only in chaos. Consequently, fighting with spears is unsuited to primitive warriors. It requires the discipline of a professionally organized army.

The short spears of the early bronze age were made longer and longer as men learned how to manage them, until they reached the proportions of the mammoth pikes of the armies of Alexander the Great. These were 18 to 22 feet long, and with them Alexander conquered much of the world. Spears were important in warfare long after

the invention of firearms. Even then they were sup-
planted by bayonets, which are only another kind of
spear.

Soldiers still use bayonets—a point on the end of a
shaft, basically the same weapon Gilgal and his comrades
fought with six thousand years ago.

CHAPTER 3

The Champions

Every nation has its heroes, who lived in what Kipling calls "the high and far-off times." Japan had Yamato-take, Germany had Siegfried, Ireland had Cuchulainn, England had King Arthur, the Algonquin Indians had Glooskap. The Greeks had Achilles and Ajax.

In their own age of greatness, which was about five hundred years before Christ, the Greeks looked backward to a time which they imagined was a golden age, a time of heroes. That was the time of which their legendary blind poet Homer had sung; the time of the great war against Troy in the 12th century B.C., when gods walked among men, when warriors were stronger and braver.

Those Greeks of that heroic age lived in kingdoms whose rulers were only a little way removed from tribal chieftains. They were not the absolute monarchs such as the Orient knew; they were leaders but not despots. The kings lived in massive stone citadels, so well built that men still marvel at the ruins of Mycenae and Tiryns. Around the forbidding stone walls of the castle huddled the houses of traders and craftsmen. Inside the castle dwelt the king and his court, their lives centered around a great stone hall known as the *megaron*. Most of the common people in the kingdom were farmers and herdsmen.

Surrounding the king was a group of men known by some name such as the "King's Companions." They were a primitive kind of aristocracy, a development of the king's bodyguard of earlier times. The Companions served as a cadre for the king's army, as policemen, as landlords, and probably as judges and tax collectors. Legendary heroes such as Achilles and Ajax were members of a similar barbaric nobility.

It would be worth while to take a closer look at one of these King's Companions. Call him Kratos the Strong, a King's Companion in the little kingdom of Leukoia, in west central Greece. No one would mistake Kratos for anything but what he was: a professional fighting man. He was burly and muscular, with curling red-brown hair and beard. He cared nothing for the embroidered tunics and dyed leather boots that some of the other Companions affected. Kratos usually wore a shapeless woolen tunic, high leather boots fastened with straps, and a grayish-brown cloak. Scars seamed his arms and body.

When he was armed for battle, Kratos was a more imposing figure. He wore a bronze helmet with a flowing horsehair plume dyed red. Over his thick body he strapped a corselet of heavy horsehide, dyed black and studded with bronze. The greaves which protected his legs were bronze; so were the nailheads and edging on his huge shield, which was shaped something like the figure 8. He carried a heavy bronze-headed spear and at his side, slung from a strap, was a straight sword of bronze.

When he went to war, Kratos and the other Companions rode in two-wheeled chariots drawn by two half-wild horses and driven by a charioteer.

War was almost an annual affair. When the harvest was in, the Companions began to get restless and long for action. The farmers welcomed an excuse to get away for a while from their dull routine, and to the traders and craftsmen, as always, war meant profits.

There was a holiday air about the whole business. The king's heralds spread the word: Leukoia was marching to attack its ancient enemy, Phocis, another small kingdom whose fortress-capital was only a little more than fifty miles away. Citizens took down their spears, knives, and shields, and assembled in the marketplace in front of the grim stone citadel of Leukoia. The fifty Companions and their servants checked off the roster of citizens, making sure each had come properly armed.

The army marched off to Phocis over stony hill tracks, escorted for the first few miles by girls and women, singing and waving garlands.

Two days later the armies met, on a dusty plain before a funnel-shaped pass that led to Phocis. This was a traditional battlefield. The men of Phocis had lined up to face them, but neither side had any rank or formation. From each army rose a great din of drumming and yelling. Every few seconds a man ran out a few steps toward the enemy, made threatening gestures and ran back, while his comrades cheered. These show-offs had no intention of fighting. It was not yet the time to fight.

Before the ordinary soldiers came to blows, if they ever

did, there must be combats between the champions of each side, the heroes, the King's Companions. Perhaps the heroes of one side would so completely overwhelm the heroes of the other that the common soldiers of the losing side, abandoning hope, would turn and run. On the other hand, perhaps the sight of the heroes fighting would spur the rest, and the battle would turn into a melee. Or perhaps—and this had happened more than once—there would be no general fighting at all, and after the heroes had clashed, both armies would sit down to feast together under the stars.

Chariots flashed out to lumber back and forth between the armies, gradually approaching one another. They were a gaudy sight, with their wooden bodies and wheels painted in bright colors and the horses hung with braiding and tassels. Clouds of dust trailed from the wheels as the chariots rumbled and pitched over the stony plain.

Most of the heroes were armed like Kratos. Some had odd, tight-fitting helmets made of boar's teeth. Their great shields of hide were painted in bold designs, sometimes with figures of snakes or animals.

The heroes, as was customary, shouted taunts and insults at each other. They knew the names and the reputations of most of those on the other side, and recognized them by their armor and the designs on their shields.

Kratos, his knees bent to ride more easily, fastened his eyes on an enemy chariot with wheels painted black and yellow, carrying a warrior whose shield bore a black snake on a yellow ground and from whose helmet, in place of a horsehair crest, rose the curling tusks of a great wild boar.

The warrior was a young King's Companion from

Phocis named Menegirion, barely twenty years old, who
had already won a reputation as a cunning and fierce
fighter. Kratos felt neither hatred nor anger toward
Menegirion, or any of the other Phocian Companions;
nothing but excitement over the coming battle. They
were professional fighting men, as he was. Under different circumstances, he and young Menegirion could have
been friends.

The chariots of Kratos and Menegirion whirled close
alongside each other. "Ho, Kratos the Strong!" the young
man bawled. "I am Menegirion the Stronger! When I
stamp, the earth shakes! When I swing my sword, men
whisper of lightning!" C636185 CO. SCHOOLS

Kratos grinned a little. "Back to the hearth fire and the
spinning, little sister!" he shouted.

Menegirion flung his arm back and cast his spear. It
rattled in the spokes of Kratos' chariot. There was a
thump and a jolt and the spear shaft broke. Kratos
growled at his charioteer, who swung his whip and
hauled on the reins. Kratos stepped off onto the ground,
turning quickly to face Menegirion. The Phocian dropped
from his chariot. All Kratos could see was the gleaming
bronze of his enemy's helmet above the yellow and black
shield. With a quick motion he threw his own spear; it
stuck quivering in the big shield and clung there, and
Menegirion shook the shield off.

"Who needs a shield when champions meet?" he
taunted.

Kratos didn't reply. He dropped his own shield. Both
men drew their heavy straight swords. From Kratos' mind
faded all awareness of the heat, the yelling of the soldiers,
the other single combats beginning up and down the

field. For him the world had contracted into a young man who approached him slowly, knees bent, sword moving in a slow rhythm. Kratos looked into his intent blue eyes for the flicker which would tell him Menegirion was about to attack.

The flicker came. With a loud yell Menegirion sprang sideways and his sword glittered in an overhand cut. It met Kratos' sword with a dull metallic clang. No fancy footwork, no deft parry and riposte were possible with those heavy, stiff bronze swords. The duel was a matter of beating down the enemy's blade, of evading the smashing power of the blows.

There was a sudden pain in Kratos' sword arm and as he raised it blood sprayed forth. The cool detachment

with which he had begun the fight vanished. Menegirion was faster than he was, more agile, much younger. He would have to end this quickly.

Kratos began to rain blows as fast as he could. The Phocian caught them easily on his blade, or skipped out of the way. It struck Kratos, forcefully, that he was fighting for his life. Each time he swung his sword, a little spurt of blood came from his wounded arm.

Then Menegirion grew too confident. He moved in quickly, swinging his sword in lateral sweeps. Kratos sank to one knee as if he were exhausted. When Mene-

girion raised his arm to strike the final blow, Kratos
sprang forward and up, holding his sword out in front
of him.

It struck Menegirion below the corselet and entered
deeply. The young man gave a hoarse gasp. As Kratos
wrenched the sword free, his adversary tottered, turned,
and fell.

Kratos knelt beside him. Menegirion's eyes were wide
and full of bewilderment; he had not yet realized that
he was dying. He raised a hand weakly, as if asking for
help, and Kratos took it in his.

"Live with the heroes, Menegirion, young warrior," he
said hoarsely.

Menegirion opened his mouth to say something, but
his face fell slack and his eyes were suddenly opaque and
empty. Kratos rose to his feet, dizzy and trembling.
Sweat ran into his eyes and his wounded arm throbbed.

He became conscious of yelling and the clash of weapons. Most of the Phocian Companions were down or re-
treating, and the Leukoians, stirred to a frenzy, were
rushing forward, waving their spears and raising great
clouds of dust. Kratos stared after them. He did not
want to fight any more.

The battle did not last long after that. The Phocians
allowed themselves to be pushed into the narrow valley
which led to their stronghold, a favorite tactic of theirs.
The maneuver had the effect of corking the neck of a
bottle, with bristling spears as the cork. The Leukoians
had no intention of throwing themselves against the
Phocian spears, and the fighting died down. Only a few
men on each side had been killed. The king caused the
trumpets to sound and his army withdrew.

The short "war" had served its purpose. It had provided a sort of safety valve to draw off the surplus energies of the farmers and tradesmen, who would now settle down contentedly to a winter of work. They had proved to themselves once again that they were men, that they were fighters. All Greece would ring with their exploits.

There was drinking and singing in the Leukoian camp that night. Kratos took no part. His wounded arm hurt, but that wasn't the reason. He felt restless, unhappy, filled with foreboding, and wandered off by himself into the crisp night. He knew, of course, that after a battle he was always listless and gloomy. The war god, who strengthened men's arms and raised their spirits during a battle, withdrew afterward; that was the reason, as everyone knew.

But this time some evil spirit must have taken the war god's place, because never before had Kratos felt so unhappy. He had killed many men in the past, but for some reason this was different; he could not forget the dying eyes of young Menegirion.

For the first time it struck him forcibly that some day he, Kratos, would be lying on a funeral pyre, while his friends poured wine over him as they chanted prayers.

Perhaps I should have been a farmer, Kratos thought, or a trader, traveling the roads with a string of mules. What have I to look forward to? Already I am less a fighting man than I was and I am not much more than thirty-five years old. Each year I get slower, my eyes not so keen . . . Somewhere there is another Menegirion who will kill me. He huddled on the barren hillside, staring with unseeing eyes at the twinkling camp fires of the Leukoian army not far away.

If there never was a man named Kratos the Strong, there were millions of soldiers who have had those thoughts and felt the same way after a battle. In the normal course of things, Kratos could not have lived many more years; to have attained the age of thirty-five as a King's Companion was rare.

In the early part of the 12th century B.C., a century or so after Kratos' time, a league of Greek kings banded together to attack the powerful city of Troy, which was bottling up trade through the Narrow Sea. The Trojan War may have lasted ten years, as Homer tells us it did, although certainly not for ten years of uninterrupted fighting. There may even have been people like Helen of Troy, and Achilles, and Hector. There certainly were men like Kratos the Strong—King's Companions, warriors in leather and bronze.

They fought just as Kratos had on the Phocian plain, with bronze spears and swords; big, arrogant, powerful men, muscled like bulls. Behind them were the lesser men, the common soldiers, with lighter spears and smaller shields, who followed their "kings"—a better term would be clan chieftains.

After the Trojan War there were invasions of the rocky Greek peninsula, and a long time of troubles during which wars swirled back and forth and the old feudal kingdoms with their massive stone citadels were overrun. A dark age settled down. When the dawn came again, in five hundred years or so, the citadels were deserted relics of another age, and the kings and heroes lived only in old songs. Greece was another land, a country of small city-states, a land incomparably closer to us in every way than the land of Kratos and Achilles.

Everything was different. A true golden age was dawning in Greece, the age of Aeschylus and Socrates and Plato. The days of the heroes were gone.

Warfare was different. Men (or at least European men) fought once more in somewhat the same way as Gilgal the herdsman had fought, three thousand years before. But Gilgal's army could no more have stood against the *hoplites,* the heavy infantry of the golden age of Greece, than a boys' softball team could beat the Yankees. The Greeks of the later age had better weapons and armor, and used iron, not bronze; but these were minor differences. The big improvement was in their organization. No longer did they depend on a few well-armed, well-trained professionals leading a rabble of farmers.

Citizens of the Greek city-states, which had replaced the old feudal kingdoms of Kratos' time, all had to undergo military training. Usually a citizen served on active duty for two years or so as a youth; he then went into a reserve corps which could be called into active duty in an emergency, and which underwent regular training periods every year—much the same system as we have today. As a general rule citizens served in the reserves until late middle age, fifty or so.

Only a minority of the inhabitants of a city-state were citizens. Customs varied widely, but in general a citizen had to be male, native-born, and owner of a specified amount of property or land.

The stiff training they took made all the difference between the unorganized mob of Gilgal's and Kratos' day and a true disciplined army. The city-states had professional commanders; graded ranks; formal commands for various maneuvers; and strict punishment for the lazy or faint-hearted. In a word, they were soldierly.

This discipline and training made every man a valuable unit of a fighting force. Each knew what to do and how to do it. The heavy-armed Greek hoplite fought in a solid square, or rather oblong, of men whose principal weapon was the long spear, or pike.

The number of men in the square—which was called a *phalanx*—depended, of course, on the number of men available. The ideal number was 4,000 to 6,000 men, formed 8 to 16 ranks deep. They did not huddle together, as Gilgal's army had. Instead, they kept about three feet between the files, so that the spears of the first four ranks could project. A phalanx of hoplites presented to the enemy a bristling front of spears, with no weak spots.

It was an unwieldy formation, but when well used it was extremely powerful. The men advanced at a steady walk, boring ahead like a giant battering-ram. Only the first four ranks did any actual fighting, and the front rank bore the brunt of it. Men in the rear ranks held their spears erect until they were needed to take the place of a comrade.

A battle between hoplites was fought by almost formal rules. Since armies of this type required a flat, open space, they usually met in such a place by unspoken agreement. Then they formed up and marched toward each other. When the front ranks clashed, there followed the slow, grinding pressure of a spear battle. It was more open than in Gilgal's day and the spears could be used far more effectively. Even so, a great deal of shoving still went on, with the rear ranks supporting the front ones. The press and crush must have been even greater than in Gilgal's battle. Eventually one side or the other would give way and stumble backward.

Observers noted an odd phenomenon about battles between phalanxes. They formed up and marched straight toward each other, but they rarely or never met head on. Both sides had a tendency to drift off to their right, probably because of a desire to keep their left side, the side protected by a shield, toward the enemy. This drifting meant that instead of colliding like two angry rams, each army's right overlapped the enemy's left, and turned the battle into a sort of clumsy whirlpool.

Powerful as it was, the phalanx had grave drawbacks. No amount of training could make it anything but clumsy and slow to move. It had to be used as a large unit; small groups of men armed with long pikes would have been all but helpless. Its effectiveness was limited to the distance the pikes projected from the front rank. The phalanx could retreat only with the greatest difficulty, and it was harder still to swing around to a flank or execute an about-face. And it could not be used effectively in rough or broken country.

Most serious of all, its flanks and rear were practically defenseless. Formidable as a phalanx was from the front, if an enemy could contrive to attack it from the side or the back, it could be easily broken and scattered.

It was for this reason that light-armed troops began to accompany the hoplites. Being a hoplite was an honor, usually reserved for citizens who could afford to equip themselves completely with spear, shield, helmet, and greaves, and perhaps body armor as well. Poorer men, or those who were not full citizens, were assigned to the skirmishing troops known as *peltasts*. Their equipment was a light shield, javelins, and a sword, and their main function—at first, anyhow—was to protect the flanks of the phalanx. The Greek armies used cavalry, too, but not to any large extent. Greek horses were few in number and not impressive in quality, and the rocky, hilly country didn't lend itself well to cavalry maneuverings. The day of the chariot in battle had long since passed.

All during the golden age of Greece the little peninsula was in almost constant turmoil. The Greeks were brilliant thinkers, scientists, artists, writers, colonizers, athletes, and traders, but they never found a way to live peacefully together. Athens, Thebes, Sparta, Corinth, Thrace, and the other city-states were continually making and breaking alliances, fighting bloody little wars, gaining and losing territory, and in general behaving much like brothers in a large and quarrelsome family. They did manage to hang together, after a fashion, when the Persians invaded Greece in the early part of the 5th century B.C. But even then their victories at Marathon and Salamis were marred by treachery, jealousy, and bickering.

During those wars the lowly peltast, the light-armed soldier, began to assume greater and greater importance. Even though the hoplites were the aristocracy, the Greeks were forced to acknowledge that a fast man with javelins and a sword, darting around to the unprotected flanks of the phalanx, could wreak havoc. After a number of battles had been decided by the peltast, the city-states began to pay more attention to him.

It was logical that if one side had more peltasts than the other, it had a better chance of smashing the opposite phalanx, so the number of light-armed soldiers was increased. The phalanx was still the solid core of defense, but the real battle was likely to be fought by the wide-ranging peltasts.

The most renowned soldiers of Greece were the dour, rigid, humorless Spartans, citizens of an otherwise undistinguished city in southern Greece. The Spartans prided themselves on their unflinching courage. But they knew little and cared less about the arts or learning, and they looked on Athens, the fountainhead of science and art, as a decadent and repellent place.

If you were a Spartan your life was grim and rough, unless you loved to fight and cared for nothing else. Professor J. B. Bury of Cambridge University, a renowned scholar on Greece, says of the Spartans: "Everything was subordinated to the art of war, and the sole aim of the state was to create invincible warriors. The whole Spartan people formed a military caste; the life of a Spartan citizen was devoted to the service of the state."

Manual work in Sparta was done by slaves, whose lives were so worthless that they could be killed on the whim of a citizen. The only hope of the slaves—*helots*—was to win comparative freedom by distinguished service in the light-armed troops. The citizens themselves were hardly better off, according to our ideas. Each one existed under a rigid, merciless system of cradle-to-grave control which barred him even from home and family life. He lived in barracks from childhood to old age.

The only individual Spartan who is remembered today is King Leonidas, who with 300 other Spartans was killed at Thermopylae by the invading Persians. Brave, yes; but getting killed was his sole contribution to history.

The Spartan army was greatly feared and won many victories, but in the end their harsh system proved an utter failure. They were so reluctant to try anything new that they were completely beaten and routed by Epaminondas, a general of the city of Thebes. Instead of

attacking in a regular line, Epaminondas greatly strengthened his left flank and used a sort of flying-wedge formation. It worked wonderfully well, but in the next battle
the Spartans were still at their old line-up.

Eventually, in a long-drawn-out and disastrous series
of wars, Sparta defeated Athens—and then fell to defeat
herself because the Spartans, although they could fight,
didn't know how to govern. Into this vacuum moved a
powerful new force, the half-barbaric Macedonians of
northern Greece. Their king, Philip, improved the phalanx with better discipline and longer spears, arming his
men with an 18-foot pike called a *sarissa*. He also disciplined his auxiliary troops, and for the first time in the
long history of Greece he made cavalry an important
part of his army.

Philip's son, Alexander, took the magnificent war machine his father had built, improved still more on it, and
conquered most of the then-known world.

Alexander based his army on the phalanx, but used his
cavalry the way the peltasts had been used—to deliver
the knockout blow. He made use of light-armed infantry,
too; and bowmen, who preceded the phalanx and then,
as the enemy came close, melted back into the ranks. He
thoroughly understood the art of hitting your enemy
where he is weakest; of making him attack where you are
strong; of feinting and dodging and keeping him off bal-
ance, and then at the exact moment slamming into him
with all your strength.

Alexander greatly refined and improved the science of
fighting with spear and sword. But battles still were
fought in essentially the same way as in Gilgal's time—
long lines of men, shoving against each other in brutal
hand-to-hand combat.

CHAPTER 4

Garrison Duty

Gaius Lucius Dervigilius was a Roman who had not a drop of Roman blood in his veins and who had never seen Rome. He was a soldier who never fought a battle. His name wasn't Gaius Lucius Dervigilius, either.

These matters need some explaining.

He was a Briton, whose name originally was Dervgill or Dryfghyll, or something of the sort; but of course such a barbarian name would not have looked well on the company roster, so when he joined the army as a slender boy of seventeen, it was changed.

After ten years in the Victrix legion Gaius was a brown-haired man of medium height, sturdy and strong, with a bull's head tattooed on one arm and the legion's eagle tattooed on the other.

He had never been outside Britain, and never expected to be. Most of his ten years in the army had been spent at the fortress-city of Eburacum (today the British city of York), keeping watch over the painted barbarians who lived in the bleak, hilly country north of the Great Wall.

The officers constantly reminded Gaius and the other

legionaries that the barbarians might attack at any
minute, but he never quite believed it. They never had,
as long as anyone could remember. Once in a while a few
of them, young warriors out for adventure, staged a raid
on farms or villages, but this didn't bother the legion at
all. Such raids were easily handled by the Roman auxiliary troops, horsemen and light infantry. Occasionally
the legion made a training march north of the wall in a
maneuver which in a later age would be known as "showing the flag." The barbarians yelled at them from moun-
taintops, but that was all. Twice the legion had marched
against some rebellious Britons, but it never came to
battle; the ill-armed, untrained villagers knew they stood
no chance against the legion, and simply vanished.

The closest Gaius ever had come to fighting a battle
had been four years earlier. The legion had been formed
up in the middle of the night and marched out at double-
time to drive off some pirates who had landed in the
Humber River and were ravaging the countryside. The
Romans thought of them as Germans. Actually they were
Saxons, the first trickles of the great tidal waves of Saxon
invasion which would pour into Britain within a few
generations. The pirates got into their boats and fled at
the approach of the legion, and all Gaius ever saw of
them was flashing oars.

Most of his life was the dreariest sort of barracks routine: drill, inspection, guard duty, training marches. He
was content; it was the only life he knew. Gaius was not
a man given to deep thought. It never occurred to him
to wonder what he was doing there, what purpose he was
serving. He was a Roman soldier. Things were as they
always had been, and that was enough for Gaius.

———————

What *was* he doing there, out on the fringes of the world, a soldier who never fought? Why did he, no Roman at all, think of himself as a Roman and look down on his countrymen who followed the old customs? What was there about this Roman army which had kept the world quiet for long centuries before Gaius had been born?

Men have been speculating about Rome for a long time. There must have been *something* about the Romans which set them apart from all the other people in the other warring tribes and city-states of the Italian peninsula. They were not an imaginative people; they were neither very artistic nor very creative; they had a wide streak of cruelty and an even wider streak of vulgarity.

They were hard-headed, practical, intensely stubborn; selfish, rapacious, persevering, slow to give anything up and slower still to admit defeat. And they kept the world at peace longer than anyone else has ever been able to do.

The city of Rome began as a trading hub. It was set in a good spot, where a north-south trade route crossed the Tiber River at the highest point where boats could navigate. It had defensible hills. Before Greece began her golden age, there was a thriving town at Rome.

The early Roman army was much like those of all the other little city-states of the time: a phalanx of spearmen buttressed by light infantry. It fought in the same way we have already seen, in a shoving-match. All able-bodied male citizens were subject to army duty; the word *legio* meant simply the "draft." Men from seventeen to forty-seven served in the field; those between forty-seven and sixty were in the home guard.

Early in their history the Romans showed their passion for reducing things to a formula and a system. They liked to make charts and diagrams, with everything fitting neatly into boxes. They divided their phalanx into three lines of battle, with a varying number of ranks in each line. The first line soldiers were the *principes*, the Number Ones. The second line were the *hastati*, and the third line the *triarii*. These last were usually grizzled veterans, sturdy and solid, who formed a human fort if the principes and hastati ran into trouble.

With this army young Rome maintained her independence and pushed her frontiers out, at the expense of her neighbors. The system worked very well as long as she was fighting other small city-states with equally primitive armies. But early in her history Rome was caught up, almost against her will, in the pattern of conquest which ended with her owning most of the ancient world.

Guided by their instinct for military matters, the Romans sought a better, more efficient way of organizing an army. About 400 B.C., when Philip of Macedon was winning battles with his phalanx, and before Alexander was born, the Romans had begun to change their whole military system. They set up an army which made the phalanx as out of date as a bronze sword.

The Romans credited the change to a man named Camillus. There was such a man, although much of what is told about him is legend. But whether it was the work of Camillus alone or, more likely, the work of a number of unsung experts, the Roman army emerged from its shake-up as the most formidable military machine the world had yet known.

The first thing Camillus and the others did was to divide up the slow, unhandy phalanx. The soldiers were organized into *maniples*, "handfuls" of men. Each maniple consisted of 120 soldiers and was equivalent to a modern company. Ten maniples were assigned to the front line, the principes; 10 to the hastati; and 10 half-strength maniples of 60 men each to the reserves, the triarii. This was the first real Roman legion. It would undergo many changes in Rome's long history, but the basic composition remained the same.

These 3,000 men were the heavy infantry, the select soldiers—to use a Greek term, the hoplites. They provided the main striking and staying power. With each legion were about 1,200 light infantry (*velites*, or speeders) and 300 to 500 horsemen.

It was still a civilian army, though. The legion was commanded by six *tribunes*, who were not necessarily professional soldiers at all. They were usually appointed by the two consuls who ruled Rome, and held supreme command in rotation—a cumbersome arrangement. The real working field-grade officers were the *centurions*, two of whom were assigned to each maniple. These were always experienced soldiers. The maniple also had a number of officers of lesser rank—commanders of 10 men, standard bearers, and so forth. It was an honor to be a legionary, as it was to be a hoplite. Only property owners and citizens could qualify. Others served in the velites (and could be rewarded for heroism by being granted citizenship) or in other auxiliary troops, or as baggage handlers or carters, or in some other menial task.

What was the advantage of this system? It provided flexibility, speed, and a much greater ability to maneu-

ver. The legions were really small armies in themselves
and even the maniples were to a degree self-contained.

The new formation meant new tactics and new weapons. The old pike fell into disfavor and was replaced by
the famous Roman *pilum*, a spear which could be cast
like a javelin or held in the hand as a shock weapon. The
pilum was one of the best weapons of its class ever made.
It was a little more than eight feet long, with a heavy
wooden shaft about four feet long. The rest of it was an
iron shank with a razor-sharp head. The Romans also
abandoned the old slashing sword in favor of a shorter
Spanish sword, adapted mostly for thrusting. Their armor
was similar to that used by other early armies: a helmet,
usually of leather; body armor, also made of toughened
leather; and an oblong shield of wood and leather, rein-
forced with brass or bronze.

No longer did the legions mass and march stolidly forward after the manner of the hoplites. The whole idea of
the reorganization was to achieve speed and ease of
movement. The men kept their rigid discipline and
obeyed orders instantly and unquestioningly, but their
formation was looser and each man fought more as an
individual.

Against the new tactics an old-fashioned phalanx was
all but helpless. Picture such a phalanx, solid and slow,
advancing against an army of legionaries. The long pikes
of the phalangites bristle and they look invulnerable.
Against them trot the legionaries, with their war horns
braying. One legion attacks from the front, but this is
only a holding action, designed to pin the phalanx down
and hold it in place. The pilums cut through the air.
Some of the men in the phalanx are hit and go down;
their places are instantly filled. More often the pilums

hit the shields of the first rank and stick there, dragging the shields down and making them useless.

But the legionaries make no attempt to break the front of the phalanx. They can't do it. The real attack comes from the flanks. The legionaries flow around the bristling front of the phalanx to its vulnerable sides, and the pilums fly. The phalanx stops and makes a desperate effort to meet the attack from the sides, but there is no way of doing it. Other legionaries launch an attack from the rear, and the phalanx is surrounded. The wall of pikes is breached, and the Romans move in with their deadly short swords.

It wasn't always that easy, of course. Nothing ever is, in war. But if the Romans had to retreat, they could still move far faster than the phalanx, and rally around their sturdy triarii—who still used the old long pikes—for another attack.

The new army demanded more training and more discipline. It is one thing to hold a spear shoulder to shoulder with your comrades. It is quite another to master a sword, handle a pilum expertly, and be able to obey complicated commands in the heat of battle. Rome found it was no longer possible to rely on the "summer soldier," the tradesman who strapped on his sword for a warm-weather campaign, then went back to his usual work in the fall. The army began to be made up of professionals, paid by the state.

The law requiring a man to own property before he could be a legionary proved a hindrance to the formation of this new army. For a long time the law was winked at, until it was finally abolished, about 100 B.C., by Gaius Marius, a fine though unscrupulous soldier.

Marius enlisted men for long terms of service, usually

twenty years. At the end of that time, if they lived (and
a good many of them did) they were given a small farm
of their own, plus a bonus. Roman citizenship was still
required of all enlisted men.

Marius was responsible for another major innovation
in the Roman army. Instead of the maniple—by then
three hundred years old—he set up a unit known as a
century which had, as its name indicates, 100 men in it.
Six centuries made up a *cohort*; 10 cohorts made up a
legion. This was the theoretical strength of a legion. In
actual practice, most of them fell short of the 6,000 men
they were supposed to have.

The centuries were commanded by centurions, who
were very roughly equivalent to captains, although all
of them did not have the same importance or dignity. A
senior centurion could be compared to a colonel, a junior
one to a lieutenant. The "top soldier" of the legion was
the *primipilus*, the "first spear," the senior centurion of
the triarii. He was in charge of the sacred golden eagle
which was the emblem of the legion. Generals listened to
the primipilus.

By the time of Marius, Rome was a pre-eminent power
in the ancient world. She had beaten the other little nations of central Italy and had thrown off the domination
of the haughty, powerful Etruscans. One by one her
enemies beyond Italy were subdued and Roman power
spread.

Instead of making slave states out of her conquered
neighbors, as had been the custom since the world began,
Rome made friends of them. They were admitted into
the Latin confederation and their citizens were regarded
as almost, though not quite, the equal of Roman citizens.

Eventually even this slight difference disappeared. Thus instead of having to spend much of their energy keeping down rebellion, the Romans continually enlisted new allies.

Of course they were beaten, many times. Their most formidable enemy was the great empire of Carthage, in Africa, which produced some of the greatest generals the world had seen. Rome fought three long wars with Carthage and came within an inch of defeat. At one point, after the battle of Cannae in 216 B.C., there was really no Roman army left. But the Romans wouldn't admit defeat. They made a mighty effort, raised another army, and in the end defeated and obliterated Carthage.

The Romans went into Greece on invitation, to suppress a tyrant. Exasperated with the perpetual quarreling of the little Greek states, they stayed, and Greece became part of Roman territory. They conquered Spain and Gaul, and the lands along the Danube. They subdued ancient, wealthy Egypt and brought the countries of the Middle East under their control.

There they stopped. The Roman Republic became an empire which continued to rule this huge territory for almost four hundred years.

A great many movies and novels show Rome in her heyday as a sink of sin, with great stress on lavish banquets and people being thrown to the lions. Some of this is true enough. The Romans had a streak of cruelty in them. Life in the capital was fairly gaudy. But it should be remembered that this high living affected most of the empire little more than gala parties in Hollywood affect a farmer in Iowa. The machinery of the empire continued to operate smoothly, even under such madmen

as the emperors Nero and Commodus. The vast majority
of people lived and died without ever having seen anyone thrown to a lion, or watched a chariot race, or even
dined on peacocks' tongues.

The basis of Rome's power always was her army. In
essence, the army *was* the empire, although the day-to-
day business was handled by civilian officials. The army
elected and deposed emperors, and sometimes assas-
sinated them. It maintained the frontiers and kept the
peace. Yet the army was never a vast organization. In
Republican days it numbered about 65,000 in the field
and 55,000 in reserve. When Augustus, the first emperor,
came to power at the end of a long series of civil wars
in 24 B.C., there were about 250,000 men in all the Roman
armies. During most of the empire, the figure hovered
between 150,000 and 200,000—and this for an army that
defended thousands of miles of frontier for an empire of
many millions of people.

After Augustus took over, there was a very long period
of peace—the *Pax Romana,* Roman peace. Peace is a
relative term, of course; there were small border wars,
endless civil disturbances, palace revolutions. But there
were no major wars.

There was no other country which could challenge
Rome. Around her borders was a collection of organized
tribesmen, fierce enough fighters but lacking cohesion
and discipline—warriors, in short, but not soldiers. Far
to the east were powerful rival empires like Parthia and
Persia, but their relations with Rome were something of
a stalemate. There was no overriding reason for them to
fight; they were a long way apart. It was something like
a conflict between a crocodile and a tiger. If either ven-

tured into the other's territory, he'd be out of his element
and risk defeat. The Asiatic empires relied on horse bowmen, and the Romans couldn't cope with them. Several
times Roman armies marched out onto the Asiatic plains
and were cut to pieces at long range by arrows. On the
other hand, the Parthians were helpless before a Roman
frontier fort and knew better than to tangle with the
legions at close range.

The average citizen of Rome rarely thought about the
army. Except for the Praetorian Guard, a legion of picked
men who served as a palace guard, soldiers were a rare
sight in Rome. They were all out on the far-flung borders
of the empire, keeping back the barbarians. Some legions
were stationed on the Rhine; some in Syria; some in
Egypt; some along the Danube; some in far-off Britain.
Certain legions, assigned to one spot, stayed there year
after year, generation after generation. Soldiers got
married and their sons joined the same legion, to be
known as *castrenses*, or "children of the fort." Old soldiers
retired and took up their farms nearby.

Fewer and fewer soldiers were Romans, or even Italians. The ranks were filled with Germans or Spaniards or
Gauls. But it was still the Roman army, working under
Roman discipline, fighting—when it was called upon to
fight—with Roman weapons.

In the 3rd century A.D. came a time of troubles, with a
succession of bad emperors, poor management, and na-
tural calamities bringing on a severe depression. But
Rome survived, and things went on just as they always
had.

Well, perhaps not quite. The rich were richer and the
poor were poorer. The barbarians outside the empire

were growing increasingly restless, perhaps because they
wanted some of Rome's wealth, perhaps because they
were being menaced by warlike nomads at their rear.
But the Roman army still guarded the frontiers and the
machinery of government still creaked along.

It was into this old, settled, somewhat weary world
that Dervgill (Gaius Lucius Dervigilius) was born,
about 350 A.D.

After he joined the Victrix legion, Dervgill found that
the most difficult thing about being a Roman soldier was
learning to wear the heavy strapped boots. Officially, he
was a *miles gregarius*, a private soldier, but nobody
called him that. All privates were *caligatae*, or "the ones
with the boots." Officers wore shoes. Dervgill got used
to the boots, though, just as he got used to the body
armor, the *lorica segmentata* of bronze, and the metal
helmet.

The recruiters hadn't told Gaius that some of his pay
would be deducted for bedding, food, and various small
things like the boots. It was, though. He was also required to contribute to a sort of insurance fund which
was supposed to take care of his burial expenses if he
should die a soldier; if he lived through his twenty
years, he collected the money. The *signifer*—an under-of-
ficer who carried the standard of the century and also
took care of its funds—told him he was expected to contribute a small amount every month to another special
fund. This fund paid for company dinners; there was
one every year on the anniversary of the date the Victrix
legion was founded. The signifer also explained about
the company bank. Gaius could invest part of his pay in

that, and draw interest; it would give him a share in a stock farm owned jointly by several centuries of the Victrix legion. The stock farm was an old, well-established enterprise, and Gaius agreed.

He was a good soldier and fell quickly into camp routine. The word "camp" is an understatement; actually Eburacum was an old and thriving city. It had been nearly three hundred years since the first legionaries arrived, laid out their camp, and began their long tour of garrison duty. But the center of the city, and the reason for its existence, was still the Roman fort.

Gaius learned to respect and admire the military legate who commanded the legion, a grizzled elderly man who was one of the few true Romans in Eburacum. He learned that the six tribunes didn't count for much; they were young men getting a taste of military life before returning to Rome for a career in civil service, and they came and went so rapidly they never became part of the legion at all. He learned that the people he really had to pay attention to were the centurions, who actually ran the legion.

Eburacum was full of people making their living from the soldiers. There were contractors who furnished grain and other necessaries. There were drovers and carters. There were the men who operated the baths which were the soldiers' recreation center; a one-eyed Spaniard who ran a tattoo parlor; a fat Briton who owned a theater where slapstick comedies were produced, along with shows featuring trained dogs, dancers, tightrope walkers, and jugglers; and any number of small shops where the legionaries could buy shoddy wares at high prices. There were wine shops by the dozen; and restaurants; and gambling houses. There was old Silius with his dancing bear, and crippled Theodoros, an ex-legionary who made a living by cobbling the soldiers' boots.

There were, in short, exactly the same kind of people who swarm into a garrison town in every age and in every country.

The hardest thing about handling a crowd of soldiers is keeping them out of trouble, which means keeping them busy. In time of war this is comparatively easy. No one knows what the next day will bring, or even what the next minute will bring. There is a spice of excitement and of danger.

It's different in peacetime. A soldier then is like a fireman when nothing is burning; nobody needs him, but he has to be on hand and ready, just in case. There is nothing really for a soldier to do, and that's when boredom and loss of morale set in. If the peace has lasted for generations, as the Roman peace had, the problem is a thousand times greater.

An officer with any experience can easily spot the first symptoms of military dry rot. The soldiers are just a little slower, a little sloppier, a little sullen. They obey orders with a hint of resentment and they march a little raggedly. The usual soldiers' grumbling, which is normal, is replaced by a snarling sort of muttering. If the dry rot isn't stopped, the army will soon deteriorate into an untrustworthy mob.

The Romans knew the answer: Keep the soldiers busy. Make work if necessary—clean something that's already clean, put in more time exercising at something the men already do perfectly. But don't let them mope in idleness. That's fatal.

The army kept Gaius so busy he had no time to complain. His day began just before dawn, when he was routed out of his bunk by the legionary who had that duty for the week. He dressed in full armor and weapons and lined up in the chilly dawn to answer to roll call and listen to the orders of the day.

Then came breakfast of porridge and bread, and after that barracks inspection. Then military exercises, which usually lasted all morning. These could be drill with pilum or sword, hurling the pilum endlessly against a target, or fencing with the sword against a wooden post. Sometimes there were mock combats with wooden weapons; or rehearsals of storming a fort in *testudo* formation —the "tortoise," with the legionaries holding their shields overhead and overlapped, to form a protective shell.

They might exercise at the ballistas and catapults which threw javelins or stones; or maneuver on the parade ground, with the centurions trying to confuse them with complicated commands on deploying or countermarching.

Then they ate their midday meal, bread and vegetables and the sour, thin wine that was the legionaries' drink. Actually it was a sort of vinegar mixed with water, unpalatable unless you were used to it, but refreshing and thirst-quenching if you were. Roman soldiers had been drinking it for centuries.

A short rest followed lunch, then more exercises. Often the soldiers went on a long march under full field pack, carrying 60 to 90 pounds on their shoulders, as well as their armor and weapons. They marched at a steady four miles an hour in the age-old Roman quickstep. When they started out, they never knew whether they would be back in the barracks by nightfall or not. If they bivouacked they set up a complete military camp, after the practice of the Romans since the days of the Republic: ditches, palisades, latrines, two streets at right angles, guard at the gates. The soldiers of Julius Caesar had set up just that sort of camp in Gaul, four hundred years earlier. If they made it back to Eburacum, in the evening there was time for cleaning weapons and gear. Then sleep.

Gaius became an *immunus,* one of the lucky ones

exempt from fatigue duty like cleaning the company streets or scrubbing the barracks. Eventually he was promoted to *principalis*, a private first class, who had certain additional privileges and higher pay.

He was not ambitious. The rank of principalis was quite enough for him; he did not dream of attaining the exalted status of centurion or *aquilifer*, the "eagle bearer" of the legion. All he wanted was to serve out his time, get his farm, collect the money he had saved, and settle down.

That is exactly what he did.

Gaius was an old man, long retired, when the legions were summoned back from Britain to defend weakening Rome. One of his grandsons marched with them. It never occurred to Gaius—or to the grandson, either—that the legions would never return. Gaius and his elderly comrades decided there was some trouble in Rome which would speedily be cleared up, then the legions would come back to Eburacum and things would go on as they always had.

He just could not conceive of a world in which Rome —the city he had never seen—was not mistress, and in which everything was not orderly and settled, with the legions keeping the peace.

Gaius died in that comfortable belief.

CHAPTER 5

Fighting Men on Horseback

Hast thou given the horse strength?
  Hast thou clothed his neck with thunder?
Canst thou make him afraid of a grasshopper?
  The glory of his nostrils is terrible.
He paweth in the valley, and rejoiceth in his
  strength; he goeth on to meet the armed men.
He mocketh at fear, and is not affrighted;
  neither turneth his back from the sword.
The quiver rattleth against him, the
  glittering spear and the shield.
He swalloweth the ground with fierceness and
  rage; neither believeth he that it is the
  sound of the trumpet.
He saith among the trumpets, Ha, ha; and he
  smelleth the battle afar off, the thunder of
  the captains, and the shouting.

This magnificent picture of a war horse is from the book of Job, written about 500 B.C., when cavalry was a familiar part of an army. Even so, the awe, almost fear, that early armies felt for the horse shines through every line. To the ancient peoples there was something supernatural about a great war stallion.

The pounding, terrible hoofs, the wild eyes, the great teeth, the powerful muscles, all inspired dread in foot soldiers. Imagine the terror of an army which knew nothing of horses, when they faced for the first time a horde of men riding such fantastic creatures! Undoubtedly they broke and ran. They must have felt that they were being attacked by demons who were half man and half animal—centaurs.

Horses were not the first animals used in warfare. Donkeys pulled the earliest war chariots. But these sturdy little animals were not suited for making war; they were too patient and possibly too intelligent. Besides, they didn't frighten anybody. A donkey can deliver a vicious kick if he is approached incautiously, but who would ever write about a donkey's neck being clothed with thunder? Who could imagine a donkey saying "Ha, ha!" among the trumpets? A donkey would more probably, and very sensibly, simply refuse to have anything to do with a battle, and sit down.

When men learned to manage horses, the donkeys retired gratefully to the farm. In time the chariots themselves—rather cumbersome vehicles—gave way to mounted horsemen.

The horse was first tamed, and trained for war, on the limitless plains of Asia. For many centuries afterward, cavalry was employed almost exclusively in the armies of the ancient Asiatic empires. European horses were few in number, and not very strong or well-developed. Besides, the hilly, rocky country of southwestern

Europe wasn't nearly as suited for cavalry as the endless steppes of Asia, or the semi-desert country of Persia and the Arabian peninsula.

The Asiatics relied largely on light cavalry; that is, cavalry with fire power but little shock power. They were armed primarily with bow and arrow. The soldiers had long, light lances as well, and probably a saber, but they depended on flights of arrows to win battles. Since the enemy was in all probability depending on the same weapon, a battle between two Asiatic armies was likely to be a formless, swirling melee, stretching over miles— the exact opposite of the static shoving-match waged by European soldiers fighting on foot. Such a battle was usually not decisive. When an army of horsemen saw it was getting the worst of things it would simply gallop off, and the winning army couldn't hold on to the ground it had gained.

Both the Greeks and Romans had cavalry and learned how to use it, although their infantry suffered disastrous defeats at the hands of enemy mounted bowmen. Caught in the open by an army of bowmen on horses, an army of infantry is all but helpless. The bowmen cannot charge into the infantrymen's spears. But they can, and did, simply ride around to the nearly defenseless flanks or rear of the foot soldiers and shoot them down almost at leisure.

It took a long time for men on foot to learn how to handle men on horses, but they did learn eventually. A horseman enjoys many advantages, but he doesn't have everything his way, either. He can move much faster than a man on foot, but he is tied to his horse. If he loses it, for whatever reason, he is in deep trouble.

Strange to say, a horse is not nearly so enduring as a man; foot soldiers can keep going long after a horse wears out. A horse has to have forage, which means that cavalry can operate only in country with plenty of grass, and then only in seasons when the grass is edible. Moving a large body of horsemen means plenty of remounts, and men to care for them, because there is always need for replacement animals due to injury or disease. A horse requires constant attention. He has to be watered, and fed, and cared for, and groomed and rubbed down, and exercised, and walked when he's in a lather, and his hoofs tended to, and his saddle and gear kept in repair. Many a cavalryman, taking care of his horse after an exhausting day, has envied the infantryman with no one to care for except himself.

A cavalry troop needs specialists in harness mending, and veterinarians, and farriers to shoe the horses, and even a man whose duty it is to kill wounded horses so they won't run wild in battle and disrupt the other animals. In action a horse, however well trained, may fall prey to sudden panic and bolt just when he shouldn't.

Cavalry is at its best in wide, empty country. When it gets into mountainous country, or thick woods, or bogs, its usefulness diminishes rapidly. It is of little use in attacking a fortified place—a walled city, say, or a palisaded camp, or even a square of determined infantrymen.

Having listed the drawbacks of cavalry, though, the fact remains that from long before the time of Job until modern days, the horse has played a major role in warfare.

Military writers are fond of pointing out that infantry

and cavalry complement each other, like a bow and arrow. When an army relies exclusively on one to the exclusion of the other, it's in trouble—unless the other army is similarly handicapped.

The cavalry has always been the scouting force, the fast movers, the eyes and ears of the army. Men on horses have been the ones who slashed at the vulnerable flank or rear of the enemy's foot soldiers, and protected their own infantry from the enemy's cavalry. They have staged sudden raids on enemy supply trains, burning and smashing baggage wagons.

The infantry has always been the Old Reliable, the holding force, the defenders. They are the ones who hang on to ground which has been gained. They defend fortified positions, and attack the enemy's fortified positions.

The two arms have always been jealous of each other, a horseman looking down on an infantryman with a kind of amused contempt. In the American Civil War, cavalrymen jeered, "Hay foot, straw foot" at the marching infantrymen, and the infantrymen, stung, sang back, "Who ever saw a dead cavalryman?" and declared a horse soldier smelled so of the stables that he wasn't a fit companion.

Many years ago there was a famous cartoon in *Punch*, the English humor magazine, which showed a crusty old general asking a young lieutenant to explain the role of cavalry in warfare. "Well," the young officer replies, "I suppose to give tone to what would otherwise be a mere vulgar brawl." The answer, flip and silly though it is, shows how cavalrymen throughout the ages have felt about their branch of soldiering.

In spite of the jeers of the infantry, the cavalry has always been the aristocratic arm. In Greece and Rome, it was composed of men of the highest classes, even though the main brunt of the fighting was borne by the hoplites or legionaries. The cavalry acted mainly as scouts and skirmishers, until the phalanxes crunched together. This worked well enough until they came up against people who knew considerably more about cavalry than they did.

Philip, king of Macedonia, and after him his son, Alexander, evolved ways of combining the strengths and weaknesses of both cavalry and infantry to produce an unbeatable combination.

Briefly, it worked like this: The Macedonians used their infantry phalanx as a kind of movable fort. The foot soldiers could not be attacked from the front by cavalry, because of their menacing long pikes. They advanced steadily and relentlessly, pinning the enemy's foot soldiers down.

The cavalry fanned out from the flanks of the phalanx. They prevented the enemy's horsemen from getting around behind, driving them back by repeated charges until the enemy's infantry was exposed. Then, like a boxer using a right hook, the Macedonian cavalry slammed into the enemy's exposed flanks, throwing him into confusion, while the Macedonian infantry ground him to pieces.

Much the same tactics were still being used fifteen hundred years after Alexander died. They were based on simple common sense, as are most successful tactics: Surprise the enemy. Confuse him. Make him fight on your terms, not on his. Hit him where he's most vulnerable. When you hit, hit as hard as you can. The more he yields, the harder you shove.

The tactics were capable of infinite variation, depend-

ing upon the enemy army, upon where the battle was
fought, and on what Alexander wanted to accomplish.
But basically he relied on a firm, formidable base of
spearmen, plus a wide-ranging, hard-hitting corps of
cavalry.

The horsemen were still handicapped, however. They
had to fight sitting down and maintain their seat by grip-
ping the horse with their knees.

Then someone, somewhere, invented stirrups. Such an
obvious device, you would think, yet they did not appear
until about fifteen hundred years ago. Stirrups changed
the entire complexion of warfare and made the horseman
without question the boss of the battlefield; and he
stayed the boss for a thousand years, until gunpowder
added another dimension to war.

The famed Roman legions were introduced to stirrups,
suddenly and disastrously, on a hot August day in the
year 378 A.D. An army of Goths, anchored firmly in their
saddles and swinging long sabers, met the legions at the
battle of Adrianople. The legions were helpless. The
Goths surrounded them, chewed them up, and killed
most of them, including their emperor, Valens.

For a long time the Western Roman Empire had been
sagging and this battle hastened its final collapse. Not
much more than a hundred years later the great empire
of Julius Caesar, of Augustus, of Trajan and Hadrian,
was just a confusion of little barbaric kingdoms. The
Eastern Roman Empire, centered in Constantinople,
managed to keep going another thousand years; but
western Europe fell to pieces. In many ways it reverted
to the pattern we last saw in the bronze age: war chiefs,
great stress on personal bravery, little or no discipline,

rudimentary military tactics and organization. A Frankish or Gothic king of the dark ages would have felt at
home in the Greece of the heroic age.

When western Europe began to emerge from the
shadows, the horse and the horseman—the cavalry—
played an immensely important part. The feudal system,
with its lords and vassals, was based on military power
in the hands of professional fighting men—the knights.

A knight was a soldier who was paid for his services
not in money, which was in extremely short supply, but
in land, which was plentiful. He was subject to military
call by his overlord. In time, a great deal of pomp and
pageantry centered about the institution of knighthood;
but in the early days a knight was just a professional soldier. Usually he had in his own service a number of
men-at-arms, who were paid in money.

There were no tightly controlled, highly organized
countries in the Europe of the early Middle Ages. The
pattern was of small, more or less independent kingdoms,
duchies, counties and principalities, with poorly defined
boundaries. The concept of countries in the modern
sense was vague, and depended on which overlord happened to be in command of an area at any given time.

The armies of the various overlords were primarily
cavalry armies, led by the mounted and armored knights.
Wars were short and on a small scale. A king (or a duke,
or a count) summoned his barons, who, in turn, summoned their knights, and the knights collected their
men-at-arms and serfs. Out they marched. Generally they
marched back again in a few months, because by feudal
law they were bound to serve only a short time—forty
days to three months.

Such a system could not maintain any pretense of a disciplined, long-service army, with rules and manuals of strategy, like the one the Romans had maintained. The armies of the early Middle Ages were usually small in number, informal in organization, and primitive in strategy. Most often they consisted of a small number of knights; a larger number of mounted men-at-arms who were not knighted and were known as *serjeants;* a still larger number of foot soldiers, more or less trained; and a rabble of peasants armed with homemade weapons. These last weren't much help to anyone. They were mostly terrified serfs who had been dragged from the plow by their overlords and told they were soldiers. They hated every minute of it, skulked and straggled, and made for home at the first opportunity.

The strategy and tactics of such an army consisted largely of a single concept: Find the enemy, rush on him with loud shouts, and may the best man win. Customarily such an army was divided into three roughly equal parts, called *battles,* and assigned the left, center, and right of the fighting front. Tactics rarely got more complicated than that.

The charge of the mounted, armored knights was a fearsome thing. The chief weapon of the knights was a lance—a long, heavy spear. In early medieval times, the lance was held over the shoulder. Later, about the time of William the Conqueror (1066), knights began to clamp the lance between their right elbow and their body, which in effect welded man, horse, and lance together into one projectile. The idea was to drive the lance right through the enemy, or if that failed, to knock him from his horse. In case the lance broke, the knights drew their

heavy, straight swords and slashed away with them. They also used axes, maces (iron-headed clubs), and falchions, heavy single-edged cutting weapons something like a butcher's cleaver.

For protection they had large shields; armor of linked metal rings (mail, called erroneously chain mail) worn over heavy padded undercoats, and iron helms, or helmets. All this weighed from 60 to 80 pounds or more, but gave good protection. An armored knight was a human tank. He could ride through a hundred peasants, armed with scythes or clubs, as easily as a bear can run through a hundred squirrels.

Individual skill and bravery counted for a great deal, just as it had in the heroic age of Greece. Challenges were hurled and accepted, and two knights would fight while the armies watched, for all the world like the encounter between Kratos and Menegirion.

Out of the feudal system grew an idea known as chivalry. The word "chivalry" means "riders on horses," or cavalry, and therefore applied only to aristocrats, since the lowly could not ride horses. It came to denote a code of conduct for the upper classes, and was an attempt to impose some standards on the crude, loud, boastful, half-barbarian knights of the early Middle Ages. The knights promised to respect and protect women (one suspects women had a good deal to do with framing the code of chivalry); to keep the laws of the church; to be truthful; to hold their word inviolate, and to be honorable in warfare. The idea took hold and without doubt did have a civilizing effect.

It led to some exaggerated behavior, however. A knight would put a patch over one eye and vow not to remove it until he had vanquished six other knights in single combat. Or he would set up his tent on a bridge and announce he was defending it against all comers—all comers of the rank of knight, that is. Or he would proclaim his ladylove to be the most beautiful woman in the world and offer to fight anyone who disagreed. Such challenges never lacked eager responses.

If a chivalrous knight were engaged in a battle to the death with an enemy and the enemy dropped his sword, the chivalrous knight would wait until he had picked it up again before trying once more to kill him. Not all knights were so high-minded, but many were. They would much rather lose a battle chivalrously than win by some means they considered unfair, and they would keep their pledged word at the cost of death or disgrace.

In time, for various reasons, the armored knight was displaced as the dominant factor in battle. But cavalry played a vital military role until modern times.

As short a time ago as the early days of World War II, cavalry officers reported for training in tank warfare equipped with boots and spurs, and protested bitterly when they were ordered to give them up. And there are thousands of American soldiers, no longer young but still hale and well, who served in the cavalry. They have never forgotten the creak of leather, the jingle of harness, the easy motion of a canter, and the thrill of a charge.

They know what Job the prophet meant when he wrote of the horse: "He saith among the trumpets, Ha, ha; and he smelleth the battle afar off, the thunder of the captains, and the shouting."

CHAPTER 6

The Attackers and the Attacked

While knights and men-at-arms were dominating the military scene in western Europe, a far different kind of soldier was coming into being in other parts of the world.

Some of them belonged to what were probably the greatest defensive armies which ever existed; the others belonged to the greatest attacking armies.

The defenders were those people of the Eastern Roman Empire we mentioned in the last chapter, who stubbornly held the empire together for a thousand years after Rome itself had fallen. The attackers were the horse bowmen, wild riders from the steppes of Asia. Let us look at the attackers first.

They were known by many names—Parthians, Scythians, Huns, Patzinaks, Tatars, Magyars, Mongols, Turks —and they differed widely in customs. Some were comparatively civilized; others were hardly more than savages. They were alike in many respects. All were hardy, stocky men who rode small wiry horses and rode them superbly. All were nomadic by instinct and warlike by nature. All were used to the vast spaces of Central Asia, with its dry climate, harsh terrain, terribly cold winters and hot summers.

As the men of Asia had for thousands of years, they lived off and with their herds of horses and cattle. For weapons they relied mainly on a strong bow and arrows, but were adept as well with the saber and the lance. They were brave, superstitious, cruel, stoical and inured to hardship.

Every so often, for one reason or another—drought, warfare, plague among their herds, or just a mass yearning for battle—great waves of these nomads would leave their empty plains and strike out to the west or south. They smashed again and again against the ancient civilization of China, until the Great Wall was built in the hope of holding them out. It didn't. They crossed the Himalayas and conquered the densely populated hot lands of India. They ravaged Russia for centuries.

Sometimes their invasions were only raids on a gigantic scale and they retreated quickly, leaving ruin and death behind. Sometimes their drive lost its momentum in country unsuited to them and they were driven back. But often they stayed; the Mongols who conquered India became the Mogul kings, one of whom built the Taj Mahal. Mongols ruled China until modern times. The Tatars imposed their rule on Russia for hundreds of years. Long after the Pilgrim Fathers came to America the Turks were besieging Vienna, and within the memory of millions of persons now living there was an Ottoman (Turkish) Empire, much of it in Europe.

They were terrible foes and great, though cruel, soldiers. After fifteen hundred years the name of Attila the Hun, who invaded Europe, is still a synonym for ferocity.

Five hundred years ago the world trembled in fear of Timur the Lame, or Tamerlane, whose custom it was to build huge pyramids from the skulls of those his army slew.

But the greatest attacker of them all was the Mongol khan named Genghis, who conquered more lands than Alexander the Great ever dreamed existed. In the 12th century, Genghis Khan's Mongol bowmen slammed into Europe, sending shivers of panic as far as remote England. Men said the great khan was the Antichrist, if not Satan himself. They spoke of his vast hordes of millions of soldiers—a gross exaggeration. Some saw in the coming of the Mongols a sign that the end of the world was at hand, and bade men prepare for the day of judgment.

The Mongols hated cities, which they regarded as blemishes on the face of the earth, taking up space which should be good grazing land. They burned the cities they occupied and slew the people they conquered with an indifference to life which was one of their most terrifying characteristics.

The men of eastern Europe—Poles, Ukrainians, Bohemians, Russians, even the Hungarian Magyars who had themselves been earlier invaders from Asia—rode forth bravely to meet the Mongols. The ignorant thought of them as some kind of hobgoblins or demons. But even the leaders, who should have known better, did not realize what they were riding against. They thought of the invaders as men who fought much as they did themselves: in a loosely organized mass, whose communications were sketchy, whose chain of command was poorly defined, whose leaders were all but independent. But such was not the case.

The great khan had organized his armies rigidly. There

were groups of 10, and groups of 100, and groups of 1,000, and 10,000, all under specified leaders. Discipline was iron hard; disobedience or even slowness in executing an order meant quick death. The men lived on the simplest of food which they carried themselves. They could cover immense distances in one day.

In battle, the Mongols functioned with the precision of a machine. Scouts reported back to the general the numbers of the enemy, the kinds of soldiers he had, any apparent strength or weakness. The general considered the reports, made his plans, and issued his orders. The Mongols had a highly organized system of signaling on the battlefield—waving standards with horsetail pennants.

As a rule, the horse bowmen hit first. Elusive and speedy, they darted in, shot their arrows, and rode off. They attacked from unexpected places and feinted to draw the enemy out of position.

After the bowmen had softened up the enemy, the Mongols sent in their heavy cavalry. These were men in lacquered leather armor, with lance and saber, whose job it was to shatter the ranks of the foe. Few armies could stand up to this terrible two-pronged assault.

Here is how it might have been when a Bohemian army, from what is today Czechoslovakia, was sent by King Wenzel to try to stem the Mongol invasion of their land:

The Bohemians wound their way sluggishly eastward through a pass in the Carpathian Mountains and onto the Polish plains. There they were to join an army of Poles, and together they would rout the mysterious Mongols.

Vladek the Wolf, a Bohemian man-at-arms, was content to be on the march and didn't waste any worry over the Mongols. He imagined them as malevolent dwarfs, no match for Bohemian soldiers and their Polish allies. He had the fullest confidence in Prince Jaroslav, general of the army, and in his own leader, the knight Bohumil of Brno. Furthermore, he had boundless pride in his own strength and in the good sword by his side, his lance, and the mail shirt and helmet he wore.

For several days there had been rumors of Mongols skulking about the army, but Vladek had seen none and was inclined to dismiss the rumors as foolishness. Nonetheless he was eager to get at the invaders. Some refugees from Ukrainia had been telling tales of the wanton cruelty of the Mongols, of people burnt alive in churches and whole towns destroyed. Vladek wanted to make sure that didn't happen to his homeland.

The Bohemians were winding through a wide, shallow valley when a shout passed down the army: "Prepare for battle!"

For once the rumors were correct; the Mongols were close by. Slowly, with a great deal of confusion and quarreling, the Bohemian army formed up for battle. No one knew exactly where he was supposed to be, but it didn't make much difference; it was always that way before a battle.

Vladek found himself in the front line, next to his leader, Bohumil. On each side he could see a forest of lances and waving pennons. Prince Jaroslav sat on his gray horse a short distance to the rear, under a dozen silk banners, and surrounded by a crowd of noblemen.

War horns blared dismally. Messengers dashed back and forth. There was an excited surging in the army as the word was passed that this was no mere detachment of Mongols—it was their whole army. Thousands of them!

Then suddenly, so suddenly Vladek was hardly aware

of it at first, the battle began. Bohemian outriders plunged down the shallow hills ringing the valley. Behind them raced a band of Mongol riders, yelping like hounds. They galloped alongside the scouts, loosing arrows; a Bohemian fell and rolled awkwardly down the hill.

Bohumil shouted and pointed to the top of the hill, where four Mongol horsemen sat. To Vladek they looked bulky and misshapen; they rode hunched in the saddle, with very short stirrups. One held aloft what looked like a lance decorated with flowing pennants, and waved it slowly from side to side.

Over the crest of the hill poured the Mongols, hundreds of them. They rode obliquely toward the Bohemians, keeping up a shrill yelping. Their bows arched and there was a swishing sound overhead, then another. The man beside Vladek gasped and slid from his horse, an arrow in his neck.

Yelling, the Bohemians broke into a trot, bringing their lances down into attack position. The trot became a gallop as the whole line of Bohemians plunged toward the flitting figures on their shaggy small horses. The Mongols, dressed in brightly colored clothes and high, fur-trimmed hats, rode without holding their reins and loosed their arrows as fast as they could.

The arrows were finding marks. Riderless horses plunged and whinnied. An arrow glanced from Vladek's helmet, and he spurred his horse forward, shouting wildly.

The charge failed. The Mongols would not meet the heavier Bohemians. Their ponies wheeled and darted like swallows. One of the ponies lost its footing and fell, and with a snarl of triumph Vladek plunged his lance through the Mongol struggling on the ground. The lance was

jerked from his grasp and he hauled out his sword.

But the Bohemians were no closer to the Mongols than they had been when the charge started. The Bohemian leaders began to shout for their men to withdraw and reform. Vladek turned his horse to trot back but the Mongols came on again, yelping like dogs and loosing their arrows.

Crazed with anger, Bohemian knights and men-at-arms, alone or in little groups, broke away from the main army to chase them. Some Mongols fell. When there was a hand-to-hand combat, the Bohemians were usually the victors. But far more often the Mongols rode away safely, only to wheel and attack again when the Europeans retreated. There were far more Bohemian than Mongol corpses lying in the trampled grass.

The pattern was repeated, and repeated again. Time after time Mongol horsemen rode in from every direction,

loosed flights of arrows, and fled. The Bohemians could not catch them, could not get close enough to use their lances or swords. There was no battle line left. The fighting swirled in disconnected patches all over the wide valley.

The horsetail signal poles were raised again, and new Mongol troops rode into the battle. These wore armor and carried lances decorated with bright tassels.

The sun was almost down now. Vladek was unhurt, but he was almost out of his mind with anger and frustration.

He knew that the battle was lost, although he had killed another archer and smashed one of the Mongol lancers from his horse. He looked around, wiping the sweat from his eyes. The sun cast long shadows over the valley. What was left of Prince Jaroslav's army was a confused mass of struggling men and animals. Vladek had no notion what to do. Bohumil was dead. The bright banners which had been flying over Prince Jaroslav were down, and Vladek did not know what had happened to the prince.

There was a thunder of hoofs. Two more Mongol riders were galloping toward Vladek. He lifted his sword and settled his hacked and battered shield. Ward off the attack of one while he dealt with the other, then—

The Mongol on the right swerved and Vladek's blow missed. He recovered quickly and caught a lance thrust on his shield. He raised the sword again.

There was a terrible shock just above his mail shirt. The shrill yells were loud in his ears and his dimming eyes saw the horsetail signals close by, waving back and forth. How did they do it? he asked himself dully. How did they beat us? He felt another shock. There was a great white blaze in his eyes, then nothing.

The Mongols, fortunately, did not stay in Europe. They withdrew to the East upon receiving news of the death of Genghis Khan's son, Ogdai Khan. Probably they could not have advanced much farther, anyhow; they were getting into country unsuited to them, more densely settled, thickly forested, cut up by mountains and rivers. But for centuries thereafter, Slavic mothers frightened their children into obedience by telling them about the terrible Mongols.

If the Mongols were the most fearsome army in attack, the most formidable in defense was that of Byzantium.

American students know less about this ancient empire than they know about the Europe of knights and ladies, of castles and tournaments. But the Eastern Roman Empire, which actually was Greek, served as the defender of Europe for a thousand years.

For all that time the Byzantine Empire fought stubbornly, with every weapon at its command, against wave after wave of invaders from every direction: Persians, Tatars, Magyars, Turks, even the mailed knights of western Europe. From their great triple-walled capital of Constantinople, gateway to Europe, they beat back the hordes of Asia. Even Genghis Khan, had he tried to push past Constantinople instead of riding over the Russian plain, probably would have been stopped.

One reason, perhaps, that we have such a vague picture of the Byzantines is that the people of western Europe neither liked nor trusted them. They were labeled deceitful, masters at lying and intrigue—everything bad the westerners could lay their tongues to. Perhaps they were, in many respects. On their side, the Byzantines thought of the men from the West—"Franks," they called them—as uncouth, illiterate barbarians. Perhaps they were right, too.

The Byzantines were concerned only with preserving their own skins. Surrounded by fierce and hungry enemies greedy for the wealth of the empire, they used every weapon they had to keep invaders at bay. They didn't hesitate to lie, to cheat, to deceive, if it meant an advantage to them.

They had a magnificent defensive army, but their best

weapon was their brains. They used them in waging war, something their enemies usually neglected to do. The Byzantines wrote hundreds of books on the art and science of war, examining such diverse topics as the best kind of wall to put around a city, and the most nourishing kind of rations for a long campaign. They had carefully worked out battle plans to cover every conceivable situation, and their generals (*strategoi,* the word our "strategy" comes from) were supposed to be letter-perfect in all of them.

Their system of military organization was much like ours today—and much like that of the Mongols—with officers from generals down to commanders of 10 men, each with definite duties and responsibilities. Every branch of the service was governed by the strictest regulations.

To the Byzantines, war was not a means for winning fame or glory, and they considered people who held such notions, like the Franks, as idiots. War was a business, just as raising cattle or making bricks was a business, and the object of it was to win, no matter how. The life of the empire depended on winning. If a general or an admiral was successful, he won wealth and honors. If he lost, there was no talk about a gallant defeat, or any sympathy for a well-fought action. There was generally a simple funeral for the loser.

The strategoi coldly calculated the enemy, planned how best to fight him, and went ahead accordingly. Very early the Byzantines saw that their most dangerous enemies were the mounted archers of Asia, and they also saw that mounted archers were helpless before fortifications. Therefore they erected a string of powerful forts on their borders, and back of these a second series of forts, equally strong. Behind the forts was the rest of the army, stationed so that it could ride speedily to any threatened point and concentrate there. The empire had the inestimable advantage of commanding the eastern Mediterranean and the Black Sea, so its armies could be moved and supplied without interference from their land-bound enemies.

Mainstay of the Byzantine army were the *cataphracts,* heavy cavalry who closely resembled the armored knights of the West. They wore helmets and jazerant armor (formed of overlapping metal scales sewed on leather or heavy cloth) and carried lance, saber, and usually bow and arrows as well. The cataphracts were formed into regiments and were all career soldiers.

The Byzantines also had splendid light cavalry, largely recruited from the Asiatics they fought; light and heavy infantry; fine engineers and a supply corps. Such a combination, together with the string of fortresses, was enough to hold off the enemy—huge in numbers, but undisciplined and unscientific.

In the early days of the empire most of the Byzantine army consisted of its own subjects, mountaineers from Greece or Asia Minor. As the centuries went on, though, the Byzantines came to depend more and more on mercenaries, that is, soldiers who were not inspired by loyalty but by a substantial wage. Reliance on hired soldiers has serious weaknesses, but it works as long as the money is forthcoming, and Byzantium was extremely wealthy. In her army could be found representatives of almost every race in Europe and many in Asia: Bulgars (who frequently fought their own kinsmen), various kinds of

Goths, Germans, Franks, Spaniards, Slavs, even blond giants from far-off Scandinavia.

There were other soldiers in the Byzantine army besides those armed with sword and bow. The Byzantines considered that the spy who stole into the enemy's camp was as much a soldier as the glittering cataphract on his horse. So was the glib ambassador who promised everything and intended to give nothing; the assassin, the briber, the one who spread false rumors, the plotter—in fact, all the unsavory intriguers who play vital roles in any total war. The Byzantines had to wage this kind of war; otherwise they would have been submerged, as the Romans of the West had been submerged.

The Byzantines simply could not understand the western concept of warfare, any more than the westerners could understand theirs. The idea of letting an unarmed enemy escape because it was unchivalrous to attack him when he could not defend himself struck them as nonsense. When, they reasoned, would there be a better time to get rid of him? They listened with a superior kind of amusement to tales of knights errant putting a patch over one eye to fulfill a vow. "What good does it do?" they asked, and the Franks sputtered in frustration trying to make them understand.

All warfare is ugly, and the Byzantine style of warfare was uglier than most. But it worked. The ancient city of Constantinople stood on the shores of the Bosphorus, unconquered, far longer than it would have if the Byzantines had tried to fight according to the rules of chivalry. Even their magnificent defensive army, though, could not hold out forever. The tides of invasion washed ever closer. The territory of the empire contracted, and new lines of forts, closer in, had to be built. With less land there was less wealth to pay the mercenary soldiers.

Finally, five hundred years ago, Constantinople stood almost like an island, supporting itself by trade, only a poor forlorn shadow of what once had been a mighty empire. The Turks, under their Sultan Mohammed II, laid siege to the city and after two months captured it in 1453, killing the last emperor, Constantine XIII.

Still, the Byzantines had managed to survive for more than a thousand years.

CHAPTER 7

The Free Companies

As the Middle Ages drew to a close, war in western Europe became more a matter of national policy and less of a private game to be played by aristocratic knights. The rulers decided it was too important to be left to impulsive amateurs, no matter how skilled they were in battle. A number of incidents strengthened this belief.

In the year 1302, for instance, a French army under Count Robert of Artois marched out to subdue some rebellious Flemings. It was a magnificent army: 40,000 foot soldiers, including several companies of the famous Genoese crossbowmen, and 7,000 horsemen, armored knights or men-at-arms. The cavalry sparkled and shone with gaudy medieval pageantry. Over their gleaming armor they wore gaily embroidered surcoats; their horses were almost hidden under flowing, bright-colored trappings, and above them waved a forest of colorful pennons and flags.

The Flemings, who lived in what is now Belgium, could muster only about half as many men. They had hardly any knights or heavy cavalry, and the army was composed chiefly of craftsmen and merchants. For the most part they were poorly armed; many of them had only heavy, iron-shod staffs.

When the two armies met near the town of Courtrai, an aide to the French Count Robert suggested that the crossbowmen and other infantry be sent forward to soften up the stubborn Flemings before the knights attacked. The count would have none of it. It would be dishonorable, he said angrily, for knights to hang back while mere common hired soldiers fought. He ordered the crossbowmen to stand aside.

The French knights charged, shouting their war cries, their pennons streaming—without even the precaution of sending out scouts or skirmishers. The Flemings had taken a position behind one of the small canals that seamed the country. The knights didn't see it—and charged straight into the canal! Many were drowned. The rest were thrown into utter confusion, milled around in disorder, got mired in muddy ground, and were methodically cut down by the Flemish burghers.

Such stupidity is hard to believe, but there are many other examples. In 1314 the English, under Edward II, invaded Scotland. They met the Scots, led by King Robert Bruce, at Bannockburn. The situation was much the same as that of the French and Flemings: the Scots were badly outnumbered, especially in horsemen.

King Robert chose a strong position to offer battle. His army, mostly spearmen on foot, formed up between two stretches of bog. Some of Edward's wiser advisers counseled against a frontal attack, which would give the Scots the advantage of a narrower front and prevent the English from encircling them. Best to circle the bogs, they said, and take the Scots from the rear.

The headstrong young English knights would have
none of that. Why waste time on these Scottish peasants?
Sweep them from the field! Like the French at Courtrai,
they dashed forward recklessly. Some bogged down in
the treacherous ground. The rest were pushed together
in such a huddle that they were helpless, and were
slaughtered.

At the great battle of Crécy, in 1346, between a small
English army and a large French one, such arrogance
led to much the same kind of disaster. The rear ranks of
the French knights refused to keep their position when
they were ordered to halt. They thought it reflected on
their courage and insisted on being up with the front
ranks. Naturally enough, this caused indescribable confusion. The contemporary historian Jean Froissart wrote:
"You must know that these kings, earls, barons, and lords
of France did not advance in any regular order, but one
after the other, or in any way most pleasing to themselves."

This time it was arrows, from the powerful English
longbows, which cut them to pieces. The French didn't
learn from their disaster, apparently. They repeated the
same kind of mistake at the battle of Poitiers, in 1365,
and again at Agincourt, in 1415.

Those battles took place in the twilight of the Middle
Ages, when the old feudal system was all but dead. But
even centuries earlier, when the armored knight was king
of the battlefield, the very qualities that made him a
formidable fighter made him a poor soldier.

Most knights were brave, proud, jealous, short-tempered, and resentful of any discipline. They would rather

lose a battle than retreat. Time and time again noblemen pulled out of battles, taking all their men with them, because of some fancied insult or slight. They acted very much like Achilles, sulking in his tent because he couldn't have what he wanted. If the right flank was the post of honor, the barons would quarrel bitterly over who should be posted there, and a baron ordered to take the left flank might very well refuse to fight and march off in a temper.

Leading such an army was very much like trying to get several temperamental movie stars to cooperate in a group scene, or like coaching a football team where everybody insists on being quarterback.

By the time of Agincourt, the armored knight was a relic, although he wouldn't admit it. New developments in warfare had passed him by.

A knight's main value in battle had been his invulnerability, and his furious charge at full gallop. Then it was discovered that he was far from invulnerable, after all. An arrow could pierce his armor; so could a bolt from a crossbow. The armorers kept making armor heavier and thicker to withstand the arrows and bolts. Heavier armor meant a heavier horse to carry it, and a heavier horse was a slower one. Eventually the knightly charger became a great, slow, clumsy beast, something like a brewery horse, whose gallop was only an awkward trot.

Knights were expensive, too. Each one maintained a small retinue of men just to serve and protect him. When you read about a medieval army of "500 lances," it doesn't mean an army of 500 men. A *lance* was a military unit, varying somewhat but usually numbering five men: a mounted knight or man-at-arms, a servant, a couple of pikemen, and perhaps a crossbowman or two.

Eventually it became apparent to the rulers that the old feudal army simply wasn't practical any more. The rabble of peasants who followed their lord to war were much more useful at home, raising animals and crops. And the knights themselves were becoming more interested in tending to their estates than they were in riding out in breastplate and helm.

Eventually the knights made a new kind of arrangement with their kings. Instead of showing up for battle with a string of unhappy serfs trailing behind, they would send the king a sum of money to be used for hiring professional soldiers. This was much more satisfactory all around. The king got better soldiers and had better control over them, and didn't have to contend with knightly arrogance and jealousy. The knight could stay home, and so could the farmer and the cowherd.

There was no problem involved in obtaining soldiers. Landless peasants; men from small villages with nothing to look forward to but hard work and poverty; younger sons of merchants and tradesmen—all were prospective soldiers. Poor countries like Scotland and Switzerland produced an oversupply of energetic young men who saw nothing for them at home, and who gladly signed up. Being a soldier meant a chance for adventure, travel, and most important of all, for loot. Even prosperous regions like Flanders had thousands of young recruits willing to shoulder a pike or aim a crossbow, eager to get away from the deadly monotony of village life.

The recruits didn't care who hired them, for most of them had few feelings of patriotism. Such ties as they felt were usually to their home towns; a Fleming from Bruges considered a Fleming from Ghent almost as much a foreigner as a Spaniard. They would fight anybody, any-where—as long as they were paid for it.

In becoming mercenaries, soldiers for hire, they were following a very old tradition. The Egyptian Pharaohs hired foreign soldiers. Some of the most troublesome en-emies Alexander the Great faced were Greeks, hired by the king of Persia. Hannibal's armies were mostly mer-cenaries; so were the armies of the later Western Roman Empire; so, as we have seen, were the armies of Byzan-tium.

The Flemings were notable pikemen, and the kings of Europe hired—perhaps rented is a better word—whole regiments of them. Scandinavians made up the honor guard at the court of the Byzantine emperor. Wealthy Venice employed thousands of Croats and Serbians. The most trusted regiment of the kings of France was made up of Scots. The Genoese, famed for their ability with the arbalest, or crossbow, sent soldiers all over Europe. Regiments of Swiss and Germans were found in prac-tically every country.

Their commanders were often men of high military ability. A good captain, who had a reputation for winning victories, usually had more applicants that he could use. Men of less ability, or less luck, served as lieutenants. Most, but by no means all, of the captains were of noble or knightly rank.

Their soldiers were a far cry from the mob of untrained peasants who had made up the infantry of earlier days. They were taught the trade of arms, how to obey orders and give them, and also something of tactics and strategy. They were organized into companies and regiments and subjected to strict discipline.

The ideal place for the professional soldier was Italy,
where war on a cash basis reached its highest development. In the Middle Ages—for that matter, up to less than
a century ago—Italy was divided into hundreds of principalities, duchies, counties, even a republic or two. Some
of these, like Florence or Venice, were nearly as powerful and at least as rich as France or England. Others were
hardly more than country estates, little patches of mountain with castles on them—you still can see these castles
by the hundred, perched on rocky hills the length of
Italy.

Large or small, they were all fiercely proud and jealous, and warfare between them never seemed to end.
Every shabby lord whose "country" was two vineyards
and a cowbarn wanted to expand at his neighbors' expense. The feudal system was never developed very
strongly in Italy, and from quite early times the wars of
these local lords were fought by hired soldiers rather than
by knights and feudal militia.

The Italian mercenaries were called *condottieri;* the
captain was a *condottiere* and the whole group was a
condotta. They were largely Swiss and German, with a
good many Spaniards, and of course Italians, and some
French or English.

If one of the dukes or counts felt himself threatened
by a neighbor, or wanted to start a war, he sent for a condottiere and made an offer: so many gold pieces down,
so much per month for each soldier, so much extra for
officers. There usually was some haggling, just as with
any purchase. When the contract was signed, the war
started. As long as it was in force the soldiers worked
(it's not quite accurate to say fought) for the lord who

employed them. When the war was over or the contract
expired, they shook hands, and the condottiere looked
around for another job. Next year he might be on the
other side of the fence, fighting his former employer.

Some of these condottiere grew rich and powerful: Sir
John Hawkwood, for instance, an Englishman who led
his White Company into Italy during a lull in the Hundred Years' War between France and England in 1360;
or Bartolemmeo Colleoni, who became captain general
of Venice and died in 1475 at the ripe old age of seventy-
five. Another, Muzio Sforza, was born a peasant but put
his ability and energy to such good use that his son became Duke of Milan in 1450. Most of these soldiers of
fortune, though, died or were killed at a fairly early age,
and few of them left anything to their heirs.

Their armies were generally small. A condotta usually
consisted of a few hundred men as a nucleus; in slack
times, their captain paid them a permanent retainer.
When war loomed, he expanded his army, according to
his need, by subcontracting—calling in other captains.
The nucleus of the condotta consisted of heavy cavalry,
armored men-at-arms, with some companies of pikemen
and other companies of archers or crossbowmen.

They approached warfare much as a professional base-
ball player approaches an important game: not with wild
enthusiasm, but with a cool wariness. Good men weren't
easy to come by, so their leaders were very careful of
them. The captains were the last people in the world to
risk the necks of good pikemen or lancers by gambling
everything on a glorious, heroic piece of recklessness or
a last ditch defense. They didn't fight battles at all if they
could help it. It was too risky. Instead, like chess players,

the captains maneuvered carefully for position. The 3,000 or 4,000 men on each side would march and counter-march, trying to draw the enemy into an unfavorable position. Months might go by without a blow being struck.

Finally the better general would get the other just where he wanted him, and the battle would be fought. Sometimes it was a farce; there were instances of battles involving thousands of soldiers in which neither side lost a man. Usually there were some casualties, but since the soldiers were all trained and disciplined men-at-arms, panic and a heavy toll of dead were rare.

There was no foolish battling to the death in a lost cause; a soldier, seeing he was beaten, very sensibly sur-rendered. And why should one professional kill another, someone he might have known for years, just because they happened to be fighting on opposite sides? Very possibly on the next job they would be shouldering pikes in the same company.

This sounds like an ideal way to fight a war, if a war has to be fought. Hire somebody to do it, keep bloodshed down to a minimum, settle everything nicely and with no hard feelings.

Of course it didn't work out so neatly. Things never do, especially in war, which is always likely to get out of hand. Other countries mixed into the tidy little Italian wars. For long, long years there was not a time when some part of western Europe was not at war, and the wars were largely fought by hired soldiers. From the Hundred Years' War between England and France (1338-1453) to the brutal, senseless Thirty Years' War three centuries later, there was plenty of employment

for soldiers. Crossbows and longbows gave way to arquebuses, armored knights gave way to cannon, and the
wars went on.

The mercenaries became a pestilence. In their intervals
of unemployment they settled down in some districts like
locusts. They were "free companies," for sale to the highest bidder. If no one hired them, they simply took what
they wanted. What could a German village do, for instance, if 2,000 hungry, greedy soldiers marched in, de-
manding money, food, or anything else? There was no
central power in Germany to stop them. France got rid
of her free companies after the Hundred Years' War, but
not until they had wandered up and down the country,
leaving ruin behind them.

Some of the free companies were nothing more than
bandits on a big scale, although they might pretend al-
legiance to the king of England, or of France, or the Duke
of Burgundy. Occasionally they set up their own domains
and defied anyone to dislodge them. A few were utterly
lawless, mere vagabonds; others were well-trained,
closely knit regiments under taut discipline, and the
more to be feared because of their efficiency. The worst
were called "scorchers and skinners," a name that tells
its own story. Even the best of them brought hunger and
distress when they descended on a town.

Of course there were many real heroes in this period;
brave, quiet, self-sacrificing men who fought hard in
battle, but were merciful and kind at heart. All too many
of the hired soldiers, though, were nothing but bullies,
and the very word "soldier" came to inspire horror.

The wars in Italy were followed by a series of bitter
religious wars in central Europe, by wars between France

and Spain, by a dozen other wars whose names are remembered now only by historians. The period of the
mercenary soldier culminated in the Thirty Years' War,
from 1618 to 1648, during which much of Germany was
reduced to a wilderness. Most of this destruction was
done by hired soldiers.

The war began as a quarrel between Catholic and
Protestant lords of the Holy Roman Empire—that ramshackle collection of semi-independent states whose emperor liked to think he was the heir of the Caesars. It
ended up in such confusion that no one was really sure
what the fighting was about.

The cruelty exhibited by the soldiers in that sup-
posedly civilized age made the Middle Ages seem mild
by comparison. One general, named Tilly, stormed and
captured Magdeburg, a prosperous city of 40,000 people.
When he was through, there was nothing left except
burned ruins, heaps of bodies, and a few hundred starving survivors. Tilly wrote to the emperor, "I am sorry you
and the ladies of the court were not there to enjoy the
spectacle."

The historian Charles F. Horne wrote: "During those
terrible thirty years, the population of the land [Ger-
many] is said to have dwindled from fifteen millions to
less than five millions. In the Palatinate [a prosperous re-
gion near the Rhine], less than fifty thousand people
remained, where there had been five hundred thousand.
Whole districts everywhere lay utterly waste, wild, and
uninhabited. Men killed themselves to escape starvation,
or slew their brothers for a fragment of bread."

Scars of the Thirty Years' War are still visible, three
hundred years later. No wonder the people of the time

came to despise the very name of "soldier"!

Seventeenth century stories and pictures show this clearly. A soldier is almost always pictured as a bully and a tyrant, cruel and drunken, dressed in extravagant clothes which caricature the dress of the time. Audiences in open-air theaters laughed and cheered when the loud-mouthed "Captain" was shown up to be a chicken-hearted fool and chased from the stage. Such swaggering, boastful cowards as Shakespeare's Pistol and Bardolph were standard characters.

In another century or so, all this would change again. Armies would still be made up of professionals; but they would be armies of nations, not armies ready to hire out for independent contract. They would fight other professionals, and leave the civilian population alone.

But in the era of the free companies and the mercenary armies, soldiers were the lowest of the low. To be a soldier was to be an outcast.

CHAPTER 8

The Sound of Guns

Nearly six hundred and fifty years ago King Edward III of England invaded Scotland, and took along with him some strange engines which he hoped would help subdue the stubborn Scots. The engines were crude iron tubes carried by pack horses.

The English soldiers had been told that the contraptions were *gonnes*, a form of machine to throw stones. They were supposed to be handier than the big trebuchets and mangonels which also threw stones.

As it turned out, the guns (to use the modern spelling) might just as well have been left at home. The invasion was a dismal failure. The invaders couldn't catch the Scots; it rained incessantly; and in the end, the English gave up and retreated. The guns added nothing whatever to the might of the army.

Nineteen years later, in 1346, King Edward, much wiser in the ways of war, took his guns with him to France and used them at the great battle of Crécy, where the English routed a much larger army of French and their allies. The guns, still the same crude iron tubes,

103

fired a few shots this time; but the main battle was between the French knights and crossbowmen on the one side, and the English longbowmen and knights on the other.

The English won handily, thanks to their longbows. The guns did no particular harm—except, as one observer said, to scare the horses—and were the subject of rude jokes by the archers and ill-tempered remarks by the armored knights. Both the archers and the knights would probably have laughed if they had been told that within a comparatively short time those feeble stone-throwing "gonnes" would make them both as out of date as the war chariot.

Guns were only the latest in a long series of experiments with throwing weapons, which began back in prehistory when men first hurled stones at their enemies. The object of all the experiments was to find ways of reaching out far enough to hurt an enemy before he could hurt you—in effect, to lengthen the arm of the hunter or warrior.

Early man had probably been throwing stones and sticks for thousands of years before some clever individual discovered that if a stick is thrown in a certain way, its sharp end will penetrate a target. Thus the javelin was born. Some even cleverer man combined a piece of resilient wood with a length of sinew, and the bow and arrow became part of mankind's arsenal.

Later, men made slings, devices which could do more damage at a much greater distance with a small stone than a much bigger stone thrown by hand. They invented the throwing stick, which served as an extension of the forearm and allowed a javelin to be flung farther and straighter. Some tribes specialized in strange throwing weapons like the boomerang and the blowgun.

When men began to build walled cities, the principles of the sling and the bow were used to build bigger weapons to knock down the walls. Roman engineers brought siege weapons to such a high degree of efficiency that they were used as models for the ballistas, mangonels, and trebuchets of the Middle Ages.

The Romans were not so inventive with smaller missile weapons—what we would call today antipersonnel weapons. They were hand-to-hand fighters, relying on the short sword and the pilum, and regarded the bow with some contempt. There were archers in the Roman auxiliary troops, but their bows were comparatively weak, difficult to shoot accurately, and the arrows didn't have much penetrating power. The Romans preferred the sling to the arrow, and employed many expert slingers in their auxiliaries. Most of the slingers came from the Balearic Islands off the coast of Spain, where the sling was a specialty. They could project stones or small lead slugs with wonderful accuracy, and with force enough to kill a man if one hit him in the head. But the range of the slings was short and they weren't very effective against armor.

The Romans were also expert with javelins and wrought havoc with them against barbarian tribes. But javelins had severe limitations as well: short range, the fact that one man could carry only a few, and their ineffectiveness against armor.

Throughout the Middle Ages, and up to the time the first feeble guns made their appearance, hand missile weapons were restricted to the bow and arrow, and the crossbow and bolt.

For most of that time the bow was much like the

Roman weapon: short, throwing a light arrow, and drawn only to the chest. It was extensively used in battles —King Harold of England was killed by a Norman arrow at Hastings in 1066—but it was at best an auxiliary weapon. Usually the archer didn't aim at his target but shot at an angle up into the air, trusting mostly to luck to bring the arrow down on the mark. Then came the longbow, which revolutionized archery in war.

In 1277 King Edward I of England, campaigning in Wales, ran up against the Welsh longbow, which was six feet or more in length, and a great deal more powerful than the English bow. It shot a longer arrow with devastating force. The Welsh archers drew the bow to their ear and actually aimed at the target. And they hit it entirely too often for the comfort of Edward's men-at-arms. The yard-long shafts could easily pierce mail and kill the unfortunate soldier wearing it.

Edward, quick to see the potential of the Welsh bow, introduced it to England. The English adopted it eagerly, improved it, refined the methods of shooting, and within a generation could put into the field a formidable army of archers.

In the hands of an expert the longbow was an excellent weapon. It could discharge 12 to 16 arrows a minute, and even more if the archer was less interested in shooting straight than in shooting rapidly. The arrow could pierce mail up to a distance well beyond 100 yards, and kill or severely wound an unarmored man at several times that distance.

Practically every English village boasted men who had been trained almost from babyhood to hold, bend, and shoot the bow, and to hit what they were aiming at. Archery was at once a training for war, a sport, and a source of national pride. Laws required Englishmen to practice with the longbow at every opportunity.

Soldiers on the Continent never took to the longbow. For one thing, the French, Spaniards, and Germans never developed the citizen militia in which the English took such pride. For another, the kings and barons on the Continent didn't want to put such a cheap, yet powerful, weapon in the hands of the peasants.

Instead, continental armies relied heavily on regiments of crossbowmen, mostly mercenaries. The crossbow was another excellent weapon, in some ways better and in other ways less effective than the longbow. The crossbow shot a short, heavy arrow, called a bolt, or *quarrel,* with considerable penetrating power. To shoot it required neither the powerful physique nor the long, rigorous training that the longbow did. It could also be cocked and held ready until the right moment for shooting, whereas the longbow had to be drawn, aimed, and shot almost in one movement. But it was much slower than the longbow; a crossbowman might loose only three bolts while a longbowman was shooting twelve arrows. The crossbow got even slower as it became more powerful. Some crossbows (or arbalests) could penetrate plate armor, but were so stiff they had to be recocked with a clumsy windlass.

It was into this world of bows, crossbows, and archaic siege weapons that "gonnes" made their appearance.

The first real guns were 4-foot iron tubes, like those used at Crécy, which fired small stones designed to knock a knight from his horse. Although they were only moderately effective in action, it was obvious that the new weapons had a military future. They began developing in two directions, which led to artillery on the one hand, and to the infantry rifle on the other.

Artillery developed much more rapidly because there was a greater need for siege weapons. Battering fortifications and assaulting castles were important elements of medieval warfare, and devices like trebuchets and mangonels, which slung stones, left a great deal to be desired. Gunpowder gave besiegers a valuable new weapon.

Military engineers began making big *bombards*, which threw stones with much greater force and at least as much accuracy as the older siege weapons. They were heavy, ponderous things, set up with much labor in bulky wooden cradles, and their rate of fire was extremely slow. Two shots a day was good for a big bombard which hurled a stone weighing several hundred pounds. It took hours to clean the gun after firing. The old fine-grained powder burned "dirty" and left a caked residue in the bore. Even so, two shots from a bombard could knock down a wall far more quickly than dozens of rounds from a big trebuchet. In 1453, Turkish bombards took just forty days to pound down the immensely thick walls of Constantinople, walls which had kept out invaders for centuries.

Early artillerymen were not considered soldiers at all, but civilians—and hated civilians at that. Knights, pikemen, and archers alike looked on them as creatures of evil, practicing a sort of black magic. They may also have had the uncomfortable feeling that these gunners represented the end of war as they knew it. And they were perfectly correct.

A gunner's life was not a happy one. He was likely to end his brief career in a monstrous explosion when something went wrong, and something was always going wrong. Meanwhile he had to suffer insults and jeers from his fellows, who considered guns to be inventions of the devil. A knight, or even an archer, could expect ransom if he was captured; a gunner could look forward only to being hanged.

In the early days of artillery it was not uncommon for a general to punish wrongdoers by sentencing them to be gunners. Sometimes gunners were drafted from the local peasantry or from lower ranks of soldiers, and held to their task by a ring of archers or crossbowmen.

It was many years before good field artillery was developed—that is, light cannon which could be wheeled into position and used against enemy soldiers instead of against enemy forts. In the early years of the 15th century, a Bohemian general experimented with small cannon mounted in armored carts—a sort of primitive tank—but it wasn't until the French-Italian wars at the beginning of the 16th century that field artillery began to play an important part in battles. By that time, siege artillery was an indispensable part of any army, and the hatred soldiers had felt for gunners was beginning to fade.

Small handguns did not win acceptance as quickly as artillery, because there was not so much need for them. The bow and arbalest, for all their drawbacks, performed well, and armies saw no immediate need to replace them with guns. It was near the end of the reign of Queen Elizabeth, in 1595, before the English finally, and reluctantly, ordered that no more English troops be armed with the longbow; and well into the following century the Scots in their Highlands were still using bows against English armies.

But once guns appeared, the arbalest and longbow

were doomed. Not because guns were more accurate, because they weren't. An archer who fought at Crécy in 1346 could have made a musketeer of the Napoleonic period look ridiculous on a target range. And not because guns were quicker, either; even an arbalest, cranked up with a windlass, had a much faster firing rate than a handgun, and a longbowman could empty his quiver easily while a gunner was reloading once. Both the bow and the arbalest also had longer ranges.

Guns eventually won out over the other hand weapons because they were easier to use. Not safer, but easier. Shooting the longbow was an art acquired only after long years of practice; and the arbalest, although not so exacting, required considerable training, too. Anybody could learn to fire a gun in a short time. The only knowledge required was how to prepare the powder; the primitive fine-grain powder had to be mixed shortly before use, or the ingredients would separate.

Early handguns were simply short iron tubes fixed onto a long wooden stock. The gunner poured some powder into the tube; then he rolled in the bullet, and a piece of wadding so the bullet wouldn't fall out. This done, he held the stock under one arm, aimed his piece at the enemy, and poked a red-hot wire into a hole near the base of the barrel. The gun usually went off, sending the lead slug wobbling through the air with enough force to put the enemy out of action if it happened to hit him.

After the art of "corning" powder was discovered, it was no longer necessary for the gunner to mix his own; ammunition could now be prepared far ahead of time by specialists. Corning was a process of dampening the powder, so that it crumbled into small, irregularly shaped

pellets when it dried out again. This allowed air to get to all parts of the charge at once and gave a much more even and better-controlled explosion.

Then the slow match was invented, and guns began to look more like the weapons we are familiar with today. The match was a length of loosely woven tow, boiled in saltpeter and lye, which had the property of holding a spark. The invention prompted development of the matchlock, the first gun to have a real trigger—although the trigger was nothing more than a lever which, when pulled, brought the lighted end of the match into contact with powder in a firing pan. The device enabled the soldier to hold the gun with both hands, instead of having to use one hand to apply the wire or match. For the first time he could concentrate on aiming while he fired.

Instead of having a straight butt, the matchlock was made with a curved or hooked butt, which the soldier rested against his chest. In English it was called the *hackbut,* or "hooked butt" gun, and in French *arquebus.* Today we use the word arquebus to mean any heavy matchlock gun of the type employed in the 16th century.

The arquebus fired a ball weighing an ounce or less, and had an effective range limited to about 200 yards. It was clumsy and inefficient; one shot every two minutes was a satisfactory rate of fire. It was also unreliable; rain or wet weather could spoil the powder and make the slow match unusable. And it was inaccurate; the ball did not fit the barrel, there were no standards for the powder, and as a consequence it had to be fired in volleys at a massed enemy. Nonetheless, with all its drawbacks, the arquebus became the standard infantry weapon of the time.

The Spaniards, the leading military power in Europe at the beginning of the 16th century, introduced an important variation of the arquebus. This was a massive handgun called a *musket,* actually a sort of hand cannon. It was six to seven feet long, weighed as much as 50 pounds, and fired a lead slug weighing two to two and one-half pounds. It had to be fired from a rest and usually took a team of two men to handle. The musket was even slower and much more cumbersome than the arquebus—the musketeer needed 56 different drill movements to reload it! Still, it could be a terrifyingly effective weapon, especially against cavalry.

Neither the arquebus nor the heavy musket, though, could be used by itself. The arquebus was much slower than the longbow or even the crossbow, and an arquebusier who had just fired his weapon was helpless. To protect him, the generals experimented with combinations of *shot,* as they called troops armed with guns, and troops armed with long pikes.

These combinations proved the undoing of the old knightly heavy cavalry. A charge of armored men would be met with devastating volleys of lead balls from arquebuses; if the survivors pressed on, they ran up against a hedge of steel points on 20-foot pikes, behind which the gunners had taken refuge.

A common way of combining the weapons was deploying a company of gunners in a front of 25 men, 10 ranks deep. As each front rank fired, it fell back to the rear, going through the complicated exercise of reloading as it worked gradually back to the front rank again. Meanwhile the pikemen kept the enemy at a distance.

Faced with this formidable opposition, cavalry declined in importance, and several military writers of the 16th century predicted that it would soon be outmoded. They were wrong, but methods of using cavalry did change.

Arquebuses were too cumbersome for horsemen to handle, but the development of the wheel-lock gun resulted in a good cavalry weapon in the form of large pistols. The wheel-lock was an intricate and expensive weapon which had to be wound up with a key; when it was wound and the trigger was pulled, a wheel spun around, striking sparks from a chunk of iron pyrites which fired the priming powder.

Armed with wheel-lock pistols, horsemen developed a method of attack which involved riding up close to the enemy, rank by rank, firing, and wheeling off to one side to allow the next rank of riders to approach. This tactic was called the *caracole*.

There still was a place, though a restricted one, for heavy cavalry; and light cavalry was used more and more for scouting. But the horseman was no longer king of the battlefield. For the first time in centuries, he was an auxiliary. Battles were now won or lost by the gunners, helped by men who still wielded that most ancient of all weapons, the spear.

During the incessant wars of the 16th and early 17th centuries, guns improved rapidly, became simpler to operate, and gained a faster rate of fire. It was no longer necessary to form infantry 25 ranks deep to give them time to reload. The matchlock and wheel-lock gave way to the *snaphance*, an early form of the familiar flintlock, and gunpowder of a better and more reliable quality was produced.

As guns improved, the proportion of pikes to guns declined. This change was hastened when the musket—which by that time no longer meant the huge Spanish weapon, but the common flintlock—became a kind of a pike itself. A dagger was jammed into the muzzle, converting the gun into a short spear. Near the end of the 17th century, the dagger was replaced by the socket bayonet. After bayonets were introduced on a widespread scale, the pikeman disappeared from battle; he had outlived his usefulness, and went the way of the armored knight.

Gone, too, was the soldier of the free company, the fighting man for hire to anyone who would pay him. Instead, armies were now being made up of men enlisted in the service of their country, rather than in the service of a lord or a captain. Like the mercenaries, they were professional soldiers; but unlike them, they were members of a national army, not a band of independent contractors.

The battlefield had changed, too. Instead of the glitter of swords and ranks of shining spear points, the observer would see only a drifting cloud of brownish-gray smoke. Instead of war cries and the thump of drums, he would hear the sullen boom of cannon and the lighter, faster crack of musket fire.

The gun had made war a great deal different—but no less cruel or tragic.

CHAPTER 9

The Swordsman

The sword has always been the weapon of honor. Even today, when swords are about as useful in combat as slingshots, officers still carry them on dress parade. In the Middle Ages, it was the tap on the shoulder with the sword which made a knight, not the tap of a mace or of a lance. Knights gave names to their favorite swords but apparently never thought of naming their favorite lances or battle-axes. A Japanese samurai almost worshiped his sword.

From Biblical times on, the sword has been, in most languages, the symbol of power and might. In the Old Testament the cherubim at the gates of Eden bear fiery swords. Even in these days of multimegaton bombs, "the sword" stands for armed might.

While the sword is a very old weapon, it isn't as old as the spear or the hatchet. A spear could be, and was, used for hunting; a hatchet for chopping trees; but from the time it was introduced, the sword was exclusively a weapon. Further, it was the weapon of chieftains and heroes.

A spear in any of its varieties, from a 6-foot stabbing weapon to a 22-foot pike, is most useful when it is used with a thousand other spears. A sword is something a man uses by himself, for single combat. It is the weapon of the aristocracy.

It is also the weapon of romance. You have no doubt read some of the great adventure tales in which the heroes are swordsmen. The most famous by far is Alexandre Dumas' novel *The Three Musketeers*. This story of D'Artagnan and his musketeer comrades—Athos, Porthos, and Aramis—was so popular that the author followed it with a whole series of books based on the same characters. Plays, an operetta, movies, and radio and television shows have all been based on the Dumas original. Dozens of other writers have borrowed the ingredients of his plot: a hero who is a magnificent swordsman; a complicated situation in which the hero uses his miraculous swordplay to defend the right, to rescue the oppressed, and usually to save a lovely girl in trouble.

Did such swordsmen ever actually exist?

Yes, they did. D'Artagnan was a real person, although his musketeer comrades were not. Cyrano de Bergerac, hero of the famous play by Edmond Rostand, was a well-known figure at the French court in the early 17th century. Cyrano, you may remember, was the one who composed a poem while he fought a duel, and killed his opponent on the last line. Neither D'Artagnan nor Cyrano, of course, was the superman that Dumas and Rostand made him out to be. But notice that they both were soldiers: D'Artagnan as a member and finally captain of the King's Musketeers; Cyrano in the Cadets of Gascony, a regiment whose members were all younger sons of aristocratic families.

It is no accident that the most famous duelists were also soldiers. As a custom, dueling has plagued the military for almost as long as there have been armies. Given thousands of young men, all trained to arms, all of them hot-headed and thin-skinned, and you are bound to have almost constant quarreling—especially with the loose discipline which was the rule in medieval and early modern times. The plague of dueling would subside when the army was campaigning, but burst forth during long periods in camp or while soldiers were quartered in a city. In most armies dueling was confined largely, although not entirely, to the ranks of officers, for a reason which we will examine a little later on.

The custom of dueling reached its height during a short period of thirty years or so at the beginning of the 17th century—the time of D'Artagnan and Cyrano. It spread from the ranks of officers to civilians of the aristocratic class and reached the proportions of a mania. The center of the craze was France, and especially the city of Paris. In one nine-year period in France alone, about 2,000 sons of aristocratic families were killed in duels.

It's romantic to read about duels. How romantic they actually were is another story entirely. Imagine you are in Paris, in the year 1608, when the rage for dueling is at its height. Here is a scene—imaginary, to be sure, but a picture of what all too often happened:

Down a narrow, cobbled street saunter two young men. Each carries at his side a long slender sword, a rapier, slung from a baldrick over his shoulder. Citizens throng the street—workmen, fruit sellers, laundresses, a merchant in sober brown.

To all these the young men pay not the slightest attention. The working people don't seem to notice them, either, but unobtrusively give them room, letting them have the high crown of the street, which is dry, and moving over to the gutters, which are foul with decaying trash.

The two young men are chevaliers—army officers and gentlemen. The working people, who are not of gentle birth, know perfectly well that the chevaliers' wicked-looking rapiers will never be drawn against them, but it's as well not to get into an argument with the gentry. Besides, lounging ten feet or so behind the chevaliers come two rough-looking men who would not feel the smallest pang at kicking a peddler or carter who might get in the way of their masters. These two are lackeys of the young gentlemen—valets, messengers, bodyguards, scroungers.

The chevaliers are an impressive-looking pair. One wears doublet and breeches of blue velvet, the other of burgundy red. Both have high-crowned, wide-brimmed *castors*—felt hats ornamented with plumes. It is before the age of wigs, but they wear their hair shoulder length, artificially curled—a job performed by the valets with hot irons. Both wear embroidered gauntlets, and their high-heeled shoes have enormous rosettes over the instep. And both carry handkerchiefs, highly perfumed, which they wave gracefully before their noses to cover the worst of the smell from the gutters.

On closer inspection, their finery isn't quite so fine. Their lace collars have a dark ring around the neck. Sweat stains have soaked through their hats and discolored their doublets around the armpits. The velvet of their breeches is napworn and stained, and both could do with new heels to their shoes. Furthermore, the perfume —their hair is drenched with it—doesn't at all conceal the fact that obviously neither of them has bathed in weeks. They would have been thought odd if they had.

Gentlemen and aristocrats they may be, but they are

anything but wealthy. Both are younger sons of minor noblemen in remote provinces of France, and are *cornets* (the equivalent of second lieutenants today) in the same cavalry regiment. Charles, the one wearing blue, comes from Anjou, where his father is siegneur over several hundred almost worthless acres and a ramshackle châ- teau. Hercule, his companion, comes from Gascony in the far south; his father is dead and his elder brother sends him a few écus whenever he happens to think about it, which isn't often.

Both are deep in debt to tradesmen, but this doesn't worry them unduly. They have been in Paris just over a year, and are fast friends. Although they are in the army, their military duties are anything but burdensome; they report once a week to the lieutenant colonel who actually runs the regiment, and occasionally take a turn at stand- ing guard. The rest of the time they gamble, drink, at- tend various social events, and get into trouble—the nor- mal life for young officers of the day.

Charles and Hercule are talking about dueling, which is not surprising. So is everyone else of their age and class. Dueling is the subject of the hour: who fought whom the day before, who survived, who is likely to sur- vive today's fights. Both have fought duels themselves. The slender rapiers, with their elaborate basket hilts, are not just for show.

Charles and Hercule turn between two gray stone buildings into a narrower street. The gutter of this alley is in the middle and down it trickles a stream of muddy, smelly water. Charles hugs one wall, Hercule the other.

A few yards down a door bangs open. There is a laugh and a shout and two more chevaliers appear.

A sudden change comes over Charles and Hercule.

They had been relaxed, careless, joking. Now Charles's head thrusts forward a bit and Hercule's legs seem to stiffen at the knees. The air is suddenly tense.

This is a crucial moment. If the two strange gentlemen turn the other way, all will be well. If they walk one behind the other to leave half the way clear, Charles and Hercule will not be outdone in politeness; they will clear half the road and the four will pass with courteous bowing and lifting of hats.

But the others do neither of these things. They have just left a tavern—the same tavern, in fact, for which Charles and Hercule have been headed. Perhaps the wine has made them adventurous. One on each side of the narrow alley, they swagger directly toward Hercule and Charles. Hercule, the little Gascon, quivers like an animal tracking his prey. He knows what this means.

The four come face to face. The one opposite Hercule is heavy-set and red-faced, dressed flamboyantly in vivid green, and sporting a mustache and goatee rather larger than the current style. He inclines his head in the mockery of a bow. "Perhaps," he says, "Monsieur will be so good as to vacate the path and allow me to proceed?"

In his turn Hercule bows. It never enters his head to vacate the path. Quite literally, he would rather die. "On the contrary," he says with equal politeness, "it occurs to me that it would be a laudable idea for Monsieur to remove himself from *my* path."

More bows. The heavy-set stranger asks whom he has the honor of addressing. This is a fair request; it must be established that both are gentlemen. It would never do to have a quarrel with someone inferior in social rank. "I am Hercule Maximien Rastaigne de Cavaillac, cadet of the house of Cavaillac and cornet in the regiment of

Gascony," Hercule answers.

Another exchange of bows. "I am overwhelmed with honor," says the stranger. "Allow me to make myself known. The Chevalier Etienne Pointarge de St. Alphonse de Bois-aux-Vierges, at your service."

Meanwhile a similar exchange has gone on between the other two, Charles de Villehardouin and Odo Henri, Sieur de l'Isle Savary. The bows are almost constant. A turnip seller, who was about to push his barrow down the narrow street, is sent on his way by the lackeys, who are whispering together. They know perfectly well what

is happening, of course, and they're not happy. The strangers look big and formidable, and if their young masters are killed they will have to hunt for other jobs.

The Chevalier Etienne, as if by inspiration, has come up with a solution for the vexing problem of who should get out of whose way. The solution was inevitable. "There is a quiet garden near by, behind the Ursuline convent," he says. "A grassy plot, a building to shield us from the sun and wind, a wall to shield us from the curious. It occurs to me that perhaps we can arrange our small difficulty there."

Hercule greets this suggestion with admiration and more bows. Now there is no question of who is to yield the path. Courteously they gesture one another to proceed. At the tavern they enlist the assistance of some other gentlemen there, who eagerly agree to act as seconds. Then the whole party moves off to the Ursuline convent, to arrange their small difficulty by trying to kill each other.

Ah, those were the great days! An unguarded word—a challenge. Then the slither of steel on steel, the clang of flashing blades, a gallant salute to a fallen foe, and a cup of wine! All for one and one for all! Very dashing, very romantic!

Possibly; but also very foolish and very stupid.

What happened behind the Ursuline convent that sunny June day in the year 1608? Hercule maintained his honor intact. He was smaller than the Chevalier Etienne, but he was twelve years younger and quick as a cat. He ran the chevalier through the shoulder, the wound became infected—as wounds usually did in those days—and the chevalier lost the use of his arm permanently.

The Sieur de l'Isle Savary maintained his honor intact by killing Charles, who lay coughing out his life behind the mossy walls of the old convent while his eyes tried to focus on the anxious face of his friend, bending over him. Charles was twenty-two years old. He left a father, two older brothers, and a young sister who were frantic with grief.

Yes, but his honor was unstained, even in death! He hadn't backed down—he didn't yield the road!

A curious custom, dueling. It's easy enough to see that soldiers are likely to be quarrelsome. But how did matters ever reach the point where men felt they had to kill each other for an unguarded word, a moment's clumsiness, or a trifle of discourtesy? How did hotheadedness reach a stage where young men prowled about looking for an excuse to fight a duel to the death? And what was this precious "honor" they guarded so jealously that they were willing to die for it?

Men have always fought with other men. Greek and Trojan fought single combats before the walls of Troy, and mailed knights leveled lances at each other in jousts.

These weren't really duels, though—not in the same sense as the duel Hercule and the Chevalier Etienne fought. The single combats which were a feature of war in ancient times were only incidents in a larger battle. When knights tried to unhorse each other in a joust they were training for real war; their lives might depend on mastery of lance or sword, and how were they to gain mastery without practice?

In knightly days there were also judicial combats, when a dispute which would today be settled in a courtroom was settled in the lists. These were not true duels either, but a rough court of justice, for our ancestors believed that might was right—or at least that the combatant with justice on his side would inevitably win.

True dueling is a private fight for private reasons and has nothing to do with either warfare or trial by combat. It became a fad only after the age of knighthood was far gone in decline.

The heavily armored knight used a great two-edged sword, meant for swinging. He didn't go about in armor and sword all the time, any more than a present-day major-league ballplayer wears his uniform around the house. But then the knight, his armor, and his heavy

sword went out of date. Men rediscovered what the ancient Romans had known: that the point of a sword is
far deadlier than its edge. The point could find chinks
in the most expensive suit of armor, from which the edge
would glide harmlessly. Armor became outmoded and a
lighter sword, made for probing with the point, grew
popular. It became fashionable for a gentleman—that is,
an aristocrat, a member of the land-owning class—to wear
a sword strapped to his side all the time. A gentleman of
D'Artagnan's time paid much more attention than we do
to fashions in dress, and he would as soon have gone out
without his shoes as without his sword. It proclaimed his
status as a gentleman. A tradesman or craftsman could
not wear a sword.

If somebody wears a sword constantly, it isn't long before he begins looking for a chance to use it—especially
if he doesn't have anything really useful to do. All over
the continent of Europe in the 17th century there were
thousands of young men who answered this description.
They were bursting with energy and ambition which had
no useful outlet. Because they were gentlemen they were
barred by custom from doing any work; they couldn't
engage in trade, still less work with their hands. They
were idle, and they wore swords; therefore they got into
trouble—which, in their day, meant fighting duels.

Hercule and Charles belonged to this class. If they had
been born three or four hundred years earlier, it would
have been a different story. They could have gone off
on a crusade, or kept the peace in their home district,
or joined the feudal guard of some count or baron. But
it was their misfortune to have been born in an age which
had no real use for them. The historic role of people
of their class had been that of career fighting men, de-

fenders and protectors of those less nobly born.

In 1608 nobody really needed, or wanted, their protection. Wars were being fought, to be sure; but they were being fought more and more by lowborn soldiers with musket and pike, and less and less by the proud, stubborn, undisciplined aristocrats.

Both Hercule and Charles took commissions in a regiment because it was almost the only thing open for them. There was the Church; but Hercule and Charles had no desire or aptitude for a religious life. Neither of them could count on any inheritance; the estates of their families were hardly big enough to support the head of the family, let alone restless younger sons.

They were misfits. In a later time they would be labeled delinquents. When a war was being waged they were needed, although their independence and pride limited their usefulness even then. But during times of peace there was no real justification for their existence.

They had nothing, really, except their swords and their honor. A gentleman's honor (the lower classes weren't supposed to have any) was a very precious thing to him. It was about all he had to cling to in a purposeless, fundamentally unhappy life.

Basically, of course, honor to them meant much what it does to us: trustworthiness, honesty, adherence to high ideals. In the days of knighthood, honor loomed much larger in people's thoughts than it does in ours. The word of a knight had to be kept, his promises had to be redeemed, his vows were sacred. This was tremendously important in a world where the knight was the soldier, the policeman, and often the judge and jury as well.

But the world moved on, and by the time of Hercule

and Charles, the knight played a far less important role in society. It no longer mattered so much whether his word was sacred or not. No one in Paris cared a sou whether Hercule's honor was unspotted—except Hercule himself. Having nothing else left, Hercule and the thousands like him clung fiercely and jealously to their honor. They became abnormally sensitive to any real or fancied slight. A knight of the 12th century would fight over being called a liar, or over a slap, but he would have shrugged off things that Hercule and his generation fought about: a friendly criticism, an unintentional jostling, a drop of spilled wine, a clumsy remark.

Men like Hercule went out of their way to seek fights. In modern language, they always carried a chip on their shoulder. They swaggered through life, daring anyone to cross them.

Meanwhile the sword and the art of using it had been undergoing rapid changes. The early duels were fought with broadswords, a fairly clumsy weapon. Both the edge and the point were used, and duelists employed a buckler, a small shield.

It wasn't long before they discarded the buckler as awkward and not of much use, and for a time in the 16th century the fashion was for a *main gauche*—a "left hander"—a dagger carried in the left hand and serving as a combined shield and second blade. Use of the sword edge was going out of favor as men found out that it's much easier to block a swing than a thrust. Swords were made lighter, thinner, and longer. The main gauche lost its popularity and the left hand and arm began to be used as a counterbalance for the right arm and sword in the lunges and parries which made up the fencer's art.

By the time of Hercule the dueling sword was the rapier—long, light, flexible, and slim, almost a huge needle. This was the weapon of D'Artagnan and his musketeers, of Cyrano, and of all the other heroes of romance.

To learn how to use the rapier, young gentlemen attended schools of fencing. These were operated by men who were technically not gentlemen (with a few exceptions) and therefore could not duel, but could teach gentlemen how. Every city in Europe had its fencing salons, and masters of the art had whole staffs working with them. At first the Spaniards were acknowledged to be the best fencers; they favored very long swords and a stiff, rigid method. Then the Italian, and finally the French, schools of fencing came into favor. They liked shorter swords and a more flexible technique.

During the dueling craze hundreds of young gentlemen spent hours every day solemnly thrusting and stamping, practicing lunges and parries. Even practicing was a dangerous business, for it was considered cowardly to use pointless foils with their tips protected by buttons. Many students were wounded and some killed at practice, and rare was the fencing master without his full complement of scars. Some of these masters were experts, but many were frauds. They advertised secret thrusts, or *bottes,* which were supposed to make victory inevitable and which they were willing to divulge for a fat fee. Needless to say, most of these bottes weren't nearly as good as advertised.

Dueling began to be fashionable in the early years of the 16th century, and by the end of that century it was already reaching the proportions of a craze. The custom was given an immense boost by King Henri III of France, a weak monarch who thought dueling was romantic and inspiring.

Chroniclers tell us that anyone worth meeting in Paris at that time had killed at least one man. The chroniclers, a snobbish lot, were talking about the aristocracy, of course. They couldn't conceive of a lawyer or a doctor or an architect—let alone a tradesman or craftsman— being worth meeting.

Duels grew more and more elaborate. The code of honor called for the combatants to have seconds to watch out for them and see that fair play was observed. But the seconds had itchy sword hands, too, and it became the thing for them to fight, as well as their principals—even though they might have nothing whatever to quarrel about. Often there were two, three, or four seconds on each side, all jabbing away at one another because Sieur Somebody had sat on the cloak of Sieur Somebody Else by mistake. Sometimes, according to historians, a duel involving six or ten men was fought for no reason at all— "As long as we're here, we might as well fight!"

By modern standards the chevaliers weren't very skill-ful fencers. They did an immense amount of posturing, slashing, and grunting, but they hadn't yet discovered one of the basic principles of modern fencing: keep your point aimed always at your opponent. And they hadn't yet invented the riposte, which turns aside your oppo-nent's blade and lunges back, all in one movement.

Still, primitive as their duels may have been, they were effective enough. No one knows how many young men died in those senseless duels, or how many more were crippled. The custom bred the professional bully, whose only concern with honor was keeping quiet about the fee he was paid for killing some youngster. It also bred the sadistic duelist, who killed for the fun of it.

It's impossible to believe that all those young chevaliers who drew their swords at the slightest excuse were itching for a fight. How many of them were caught up in a custom they hated, but which they didn't have the courage to defy? How many had nightmares in which they were facing a man who could easily kill them? How many were there who would far rather have spent their days in study, perhaps, or farming?

The custom got so far out of hand that Louis XIII's prime minister, the great Cardinal Richelieu, decided to stamp it out. He swore that he would execute the next nobleman he caught dueling. In 1627 the Count de Boutteville, a renowned duelist, defied the cardinal's edict and fought a duel. Richelieu had both him and his second, the Count de Chapelles, beheaded. His action caused an uproar, but it considerably dampened the ardor of the duelists and marked the beginning of the decline of dueling as a favorite sport. Many duels were fought during the long reign of Louis XIV, but the craze had passed, and near the end of his reign Louis expressed his satisfaction at the comparative scarcity of duels.

Even so, the custom died hard. Dueling with pistols was popular all through the 18th century, and during the reign of George III of England (1760–1820) there were 172 duels recorded in that country, of which more than half resulted in someone's death. How many unrecorded duels there were, no one knows. In many ways a pistol duel is more dangerous than one with swords, because a lead ball inflicts a frightful wound and is much more likely to become infected than a wound inflicted by a sword.

Duels were common during the Napoleonic era, especially among military men. Oddly enough, they were also popular in democratic America before the Civil War. Everyone knows about the famous duel in which Aaron Burr killed Alexander Hamilton. Young Southern gentlemen made a practice of "calling out" an adversary for some real or imagined insult. Every aristocratic family had its case of fine imported dueling pistols, and most Southern cities boasted their "dueling oaks" or some favorite spot for such affairs of honor.

The custom was practically stamped out in England after a few years of Victoria's reign, although it lingered in continental Europe until modern times. Hungarian army officers were famous for the terrible duels they fought with curved sabers. Students at Heidelberg University in Germany dueled as a sport and were often severely wounded and occasionally killed. Up until World War II the German army legalized duels among its officers, although under strict regulation and limitation. Even today, duels between politicians of Latin countries are fairly common.

History and literature are full of accounts of weird duels, many of them true. The pirate chieftain of Louisiana, Jean Lafitte, and one of his lieutenants are said to have fought a "duel" in which both sat on a keg of powder with a lighted fuse. The one who ran first was the loser! There have been duels in which the antagonists chose from a pair of pistols, only one of which was loaded. There were duels on the American frontier where both parties were put on a small island, each with a gun with one bullet, and a knife. There have been duels in which two men wrestled for possession of one knife, and a terrible form of dueling in which both had knives and each had one end of a handkerchief in his teeth—it was forbidden to drop the handkerchief.

But these are freaks. The old custom of dueling is dead, and let us hope it stays dead. It is thrilling to read about the exploits of D'Artagnan or Cyrano, but you can be grateful you didn't live in those days.

CHAPTER 10

Fighting by the Rule Book

Upper-class Europeans of the 18th century were a highly civilized lot. They took great delight in reminding themselves that they lived in an age of enlightenment, and shook their heads at the rude, boorish manners of their immediate ancestors. The arts, the sciences, and philosophy all flourished, and modes and manners were polished to a degree of elaborateness they had never attained before—and have not equaled since.

Even the wars of the 18th century were civilized. Barbarities like those which had occurred in the Thirty Years' War, only a century earlier, were no longer tolerated in the age of enlightenment. The leaders in modes and culture liked to remind one another of what the great King Frederick of Prussia had said: "Wars are fought between rulers and not between peoples. The civilian population of a country should not even be aware that a state of war exists."

Wars in the 18th century were usually political devices, entered into to gain some limited objective: a trade advantage, an alliance, an important port city. Nobody

134

really hated the enemy. War or no war, Englishmen and Frenchmen carried on a thriving business in smuggling woolens and wines, and no one thought the worse of them for it. Soldiers did not devastate a countryside, or massacre noncombatants, as soldiers had done in previous centuries. They generally brought along their own food or bought it, even in an enemy country.

A war was conducted with great ceremony, and the generals followed rules which were adhered to by both sides. A siege, for instance, was carried out almost as if there were a referee standing by, ready to blow the whistle if someone committed a foul. Certain moves were made by the besiegers, to be answered by certain moves by the besieged. The commander of a besieged fortress was expected to resist as long as there was reasonable hope that the enemy might get tired and go home, or that somebody would come to his aid with a relieving army. If nobody came by the time a hole was punched in the walls, he was expected to surrender. It was his duty, and no one thought any the worse of him for doing it.

The besiegers proceeded methodically according to principles laid down by military engineers. They dug a trench encircling the fort, then crept forward in zigzag approach trenches to dig another ring trench, and so on. Their cannon meanwhile kept up a brisk exchange of fire with the people in the fort. There were storming parties by the attackers and sallies by the defenders, and after a while both commanders knew whether or not the siege would succeed. It was something like a chess game in which one of the players, seeing he can't possibly win, resigns before he is checkmated.

If the defending general surrendered on schedule, he was allowed to march out with bands playing and flags waving—"the honors of war." Often the defeated force was allowed to keep one cannon, as a symbol that it was not really beaten at all and was giving up only to avoid bloodshed. Any commander who kept on fighting after a "reasonable" time was breaking the rules, and he was usually hanged by the victor.

There were echoes of the old condottieri days in 18th century warfare. Armies made endless marches and countermarches as the generals, always going by the rule book, tried to maneuver the enemy into a bad situation. The campaign season began in the spring, when roads dried out; and wars were called off, or at least ground to a halt, when autumn rains began. It was foolish to try to march through mud; much better to sit quietly in some friendly town and start all over again the following May.

This leisurely kind of limited war met with approval from everyone. In 1760 a British general wrote: "It is the business of a general always to get the better of his enemy, but not always to fight, and if he can do his business without fighting, so much the better."

It all sounds very civilized and enlightened, and reading accounts of battles fought in those days seems to bear this out: "Coulaincourt advanced his left and exchanged a brisk fire with Von Metschke's right flank, retiring, however, when Holzmann brought his batteries into action." . . . "Two brigades under General Delacroix, deploying briskly, succeeded in pushing Count Hirsch from the field." . . . A battle sounds like a healthful exercise, to be followed by a hot shower and a change of clothes.

Well, 18th century battles weren't all that healthful or

enlightened. It would be worth while to take a closer look at a typical one.

Picture a low hill in what is today Belgium on a bright May day in the year 1745. From a vantage point near the top, you can look down upon a sweep of beautiful farming country, with neat villages scattered here and there. But a great battle is about to be fought near one of the villages, Fontenoy. The battle is an incident in the War of the Austrian Succession, which began in a squabble between Frederick the Great and the Empress Maria Theresa of Austria, and spread to involve other countries.

At the moment the French are besieging the Flemish fortress of Tournai. Their enemies—English, German, and Dutch allies—have sent an army to relieve the siege, and the French have sent along another army to beat them off.

The allies, numbering about 46,000 soldiers, are under the command of the Duke of Cumberland, the son of George II of England. The French number about 52,000; they are under the command of Marshal Saxe.

This Belgian country is old in war. It has been fought over since Roman days and it will be fought over many times more. In the midst of the marching soldiers, peasants are at work in their fields, apparently paying no attention whatever to the battle taking shape. Cows are grazing placidly.

The French army is formed up in a shallow basin between two rises of ground. It is a brilliant sight—long lines of men in white coats, standing in precise lines, with countless flags flying. Off to the French left, the northeast, is a small fort of the kind known as a redoubt. It stands at the edge of an arm of forest.

Here come the allies. They are an equally brilliant

sight: long lines of British in their red coats, Dutchmen in blue, Germans in green or black. The lines wind sluggishly, like vast caterpillars, along the roads and through the fields. They, too, have banners flying. The sun glances from the tips of their bayonets.

Above the rattle of drums you can hear a thin piping of fifes. It would never do to send soldiers into battle without martial music. The generals of both sides, with their aides-de-camp and messengers, sit on horseback in places where they can see most of the battlefield. Messengers keep riding off at full speed to various commanders.

The Duke of Cumberland plans to swing some of his horse and foot around and smash into the French left flank. Before he can do that, though, he has to knock out the redoubt at the edge of the woods. Some of the messengers he dispatches are carrying orders for a brigade to attack the fort and take it out of action. A detachment of redcoats and their allies begin marching toward the redoubt.

All of this takes a great deal of time. The soldiers march slowly, at a rigidly controlled pace. The sergeants, carrying their *spontoons*—a sort of short spear, their badge of office—keep the ranks and files straight. Long lines of soldiers join other lines, meet and flow apart, start and halt again, as if they were taking part in some giant minuet.

From the top of the hill it is hard to realize that those tiny figures, all dressed alike, are men—hot, sweating, cursing men, who know they are going to fight a battle but don't know how or when, who can't see much but the men directly in front of them, who for the most part are probably frightened. To you they look like dolls, little dolls in gay uniforms, scattered around on a green carpet.

There are some puffs of smoke, yells, and some firing

from the men sent to take the redoubt. A few cannon are toiling toward it, pulled by teams of horses. But most of the brigade sent after the redoubt just stands there without doing anything. A whole procession of messengers from the duke doesn't stir them into activity.

Now, apparently, the duke abandons his idea of a flank attack and is going to order his army straight ahead, right into the cannon and musket fire of the long lines of Frenchmen. But first he must get his army out of marching order and deployed into position for attack; and he must do this within sight of the enemy. He sends some cavalry ahead to form a screen behind which his infantry can deploy. The horses trot forward; a brave sight, with the white crests of their riders' helmets flying, their sabers and cuirasses gleaming. They move through the close files of infantrymen and out into the open space between the two armies.

And the slaughter begins. You hear a dull thud, then another, and another. Clouds of dirty brown smoke begin to drift toward the blue sky. It is the French cannon, firing into the cavalrymen. You can see the cannonballs rise and fall—they seem to travel as slowly as a kicked football—and smash into the horsemen. The cavalry can't stand up to it. Bugles sound with a tinny blare; they are being ordered back.

Now the duke commands his infantry to move forward. They must advance into that cannon fire and form up into a line of battle by themselves, with the first men forming a screen for the ones who follow.

The infantry winds forward at the same slow, steady pace, drums rattling and fifes shrilling. The shot keeps coming. Smoke puffs begin to form a low-lying, greasy-looking cloud. Sometimes the shot misses, and bounces along the ground or plows up a long furrow. More often the solid iron shot, weighing 8 to 16 pounds, slams into the ranks of the foot soldiers with frightful effect.

Without faltering, the infantry moves forward and deploys. Over to your left, Dutch soldiers are advancing against the village of Fontenoy itself, but they don't seem to be having much success. There are countless smoke puffs from musket volleys, but the attack is bogged down and wavers aimlessly back and forth.

Finally the 14,000 British soldiers are ready—or nearly ready. They still stand, rigid and motionless, while their sergeants straighten up their ranks, just as if they were on parade in London. Officers go up and down, inspecting them, pausing to say a word to some.

Every few minutes a cannonball smacks into the ranks. The soldiers form up again, stepping forward to fill the vacant places.

Still slowly, still in precise lines, still with flags and drums and fifes, they move off toward the French. Now they are being fired on from both sides. In spite of their iron training they begin to inch toward the center, away from the rain of death that is pouring at them from left and right.

Just as disciplined, in just as well-ordered a formation, the French step forward to meet them. The cannon die down; the two armies are only about a hundred paces apart.

A British officer in front of the lines now commits a grave breach of discipline. He runs forward a few steps, waves his hat, and pulls out a flask of brandy. With a ceremonial salute he drinks to the enemy and calls for

three cheers for the French. The cheers—a little ragged—
are given by his men. The cheers are answered, even more
raggedly, from the French lines.

Later, this will become a legend and it will be said that
the English officer, Captain Charles Lord Hay, invited
the French to fire first, and the French declined. The
legend may be true.

Still slowly, still deliberately, the English raise their
muskets and point them at the French lines. The command "Give fire!" is shouted and there is a rolling crash
—the dreaded English volley.

Eight hundred and ten Frenchmen fall dead in that
instant.

Precisely and automatically the British go through the
complicated exercise of reloading. The sergeants shout
the manual: "Handle cartridge! Prime! Load! Draw ramrods! Ram cartridge! Return ramrods! Make ready!
Present! Give fire!" The soldiers cannot hear the commands, but their training is such that they carry them
out in almost perfect unison.

Another volley. The air is filled with smoke and fumes.
For the first time the Frenchmen waver and their perfect
lines are ragged.

The Englishmen press forward, still loading and firing.
French cavalry gallops up but cannot get through the
press of men on foot. Then the French Marshal Saxe—
he is ill and old, and can hardly sit his horse—orders the
cannon into action. At point-blank range they open up
on the slowly advancing British ranks.

For all their discipline, the red-coated British cannot
face this. They falter and fall back. The cavalry rides up
again, and the white-coated French infantry, seeing the
enemy reel, runs forward with bayonets fixed.

The British retire slowly. There are not nearly so many of them as there were a few moments ago. Their ranks are not so tidy. But they do not break and run. The sergeants, those that are left, keep chanting the ritual for loading and firing, and the muskets flash again and again. The Frenchmen have a good deal of respect for the stubborn enemy and don't follow too closely. The redcoats finally make it back to the spot from which they started.

The Battle of Fontenoy is over. The British have lost 7,500 men, the French 7,200. Many British regiments are so depleted that they will have to be built up again almost from scratch. But still the British people back home will hail Fontenoy as a glorious action.

On that same day—May 11, 1745—a recruit named Harry Jenkins put in his first day of drill as a soldier in the British army.

There were 16 recruits, including Harry. They had been brought to an old inn named "The Jolly Boys" in Surrey, in the south of England, where they were quartered in a hayloft over the big stables. England did not believe in furnishing regular barracks for her soldiers. The English liked to pretend to themselves that their army was all citizen militia, and that therefore there was no need for barracks for a regular army. They preferred to pay innkeepers to house them, or billet them in private homes.

The 16 recruits had spent an exhausting morning learning how to stand the way a soldier stands. It was tiresome and unnatural and made their legs and shoulders ache, but most of them had grasped the idea at last. Now, after a midday meal of bread and cheese, they were beginning to learn how to march.

Eight of them were trying to do it with their ankles strapped together; the strap was just long enough to allow them to take a step of exactly 28 inches, the standard infantry pace. The short ones had to stretch to make it, while the tall ones were brought up with a jerk at the end of each step. The other eight, quicker to learn or luckier than their fellows, had not been strapped. They were marching, awkwardly, in two ranks of four, beside a row of pegs set into the earth 28 inches apart, trying to bring their heels down exactly even with the pegs.

Their drillmaster was a soldier in white breeches, white gaiters, white shirt, and red waistcoat. He chanted "HUP - two - HUP - two" in a nasal voice as he marched up and down, and he carried a switch with which he cut viciously at the calves of those who stumbled or missed step.

The recruits were soldiers, although they had not yet been issued uniforms or weapons. Each had sworn an oath and "taken the king's shilling" to bind it. They had all been promised an enlistment bounty of four golden sovereigns each, but none of them had received it yet. About half of the recruits were townsmen; the others were country bred, red-faced and rawboned.

They were not machines yet but in a few months they would be, ready for whatever battles they would be called upon to fight. Their enemies would be the French; "enemy" and "French" were almost synonyms in Britain at the time. The fighting might come in the Low Countries, or in the wilderness of North America, or halfway around the world in mysterious India.

When they had become machines they would do

exactly as they were told, exactly as they had been taught how to do it. It didn't matter what the command was. If they were ordered to march at slow place against the mouths of massed cannon, the sergeants would dress the ranks carefully and they would march. No matter if everyone, from the drummer boy to the colonel, knew that the order was foolish and obeying it meant suicide. "Theirs not to reason why," as the poet Tennyson would say about a similar situation a century later. "Theirs but to do and die."

For this they were paid eightpence a day, minus certain fees deducted by the army—fees for the surgeon and the paymaster, for instance. Minus also certain small extortions, illegal but inevitable, which went to the non-commissioned officers and even to the commissioned officers.

Eightpence a day was the same wage which Queen Elizabeth had paid her soldiers nearly two hundred years earlier. Not for another forty years would a soldier get the magnificent sum of a shilling, fourteen cents, a day.

The eight recruits learning to march with their ankles strapped together were a good representative cross section of the men who made up the British army—for that matter, most of the armies of Europe—in that enlightened 18th century.

Of the eight, one was a Somersetshire farmhand in trouble for poaching, who had been allowed to join the army instead of being sent to prison. One was a petty criminal from Bristol. One was a Yorkshire sheepherder; he had fallen afoul of the local squire, beaten him severely, and wisely run away. One was a tailor, overwhelmed by debts. Two were not English at all: a Scot fleeing some clan feud in the Highlands, and an Irishman wanted in Wexford for a tavern killing. One was a rather delicate young man who had escaped from a tyrannical father. The last was 18-year-old Harry Jenkins, born and raised in an East London slum, who had joined the army as an alternative to starvation.

Already they were beginning to feel the gulf that separated them from the civilian population. Farmers and drovers in the inn ignored them pointedly. Girls in the village averted their eyes and crossed to the other side of the street when they saw soldiers coming. After a while, when they had been made into machines, Harry and the others would not care, but for a while it would hurt.

A soldier was no longer a scorcher and skinner, a creature to be dreaded. Most people looked down on him with something not far from contempt. No respectable young man took the king's shilling in England, even though there was a war being fought. (Officers were different. It cost money to be an officer; you bought your commission and you bought promotion. Only gentlemen could be officers, with the rarest of exceptions, and—again with rare exceptions—no gentleman would serve in the ranks.)

In that age of enlightenment the soldiers had to be machines, trained to perform their duties without thinking. Their battles were brutal. Considering the number of men engaged, an extraordinary amount of blood was spilled.

At the Battle of Prague in 1756, during the Seven Years' War, the Prussians suffered 11,740 casualties in two hours of fighting—more than one fifth of their entire army. The Austrians, their enemies, lost 10,000 killed and wounded and 4,275 prisoners. In World War II, such a percentage of casualties would have been a frightful disaster. It was routine in the 18th century.

At the Battle of Zorndorf, in 1758, of 36,000 men in action the Prussians suffered 12,500 casualties, plus 1,000 taken prisoner or missing, nearly 37 per cent of their effectives. The Russians lost 21,000 out of 42,000—just half! Of six British regiments totaling 4,434 men which took part in the Battle of Minden (1759), 1,330 were casualties—nearly one third.

Furthermore, a much smaller percentage of wounded survived in those days. The lead musket balls inflicted terrible wounds. Surgery was primitive, and medicine even more so. A trifling wound was likely to become infected and prove fatal. Shattered arms or legs, which today could be saved easily, had to be amputated then —without anesthetics, of course—and the stump treated by coating it with hot tar. Only a small percentage of amputees avoided falling victim to gangrene.

Such terrible casualties were inevitable, given the rule book by which battles were fought. The usual tactics were similar to those used at Fontenoy: Soften up the enemy with cannon fire. Advance in formation. When you get within musket range (the shorter the range, the better—preferably under 50 yards) fire by volleys. When the enemy wavers, charge home with the bayonet and rout him.

Soldiers were the same two hundred years ago as they are now. They knew perfectly well, when they were ordered to advance at slow step against an enemy, that the chances were large they would never survive. They were rarely enthusiastic at such a prospect, yet the rule book said it had to be done. Discipline was brutal. The

harshest kinds of punishment were decreed for the smallest disobedience, or even for a momentary hesitation in
carrying out a command. Floggings were everyday
occurrences and death sentences not at all uncommon.

Even so, soldiers deserted wholesale from every army,
though they knew the penalty—death—and knew that the
chances of winning free were small. Frederick the Great,
the king who didn't think civilians should even know a
war was being fought, believed he had the answer to
the desertion problem: Make the soldiers fear their officers even more than they fear the enemy. This Spartan
discipline was not a success, however. The harsher the
discipline, the more desertions there were, and the pitiless Prussian army had the highest desertion rate of all.

In those days the gulf between an officer and a man
in the ranks was enormous. Rarely did even junior officers have any direct contact with enlisted men, although
the sergeants acted as go-betweens. Noncommissioned
officers ruled the privates like despots, and could be sure
of being backed up by their officers. A good sergeant
was a godsend to the men under him; a bad one, a tyrant
or a thief, could make life insupportable.

Far too many officers knew little or nothing about their
job; they hardly ever even put in an appearance at drill
or parade, and weren't interested in the welfare of their
men. Some did care and worked hard to benefit the soldiers under their command, but there were few standards: Captain A might be a good soldier and a born
leader, while Captain B might be an incompetent, cruel
tyrant.

In France, in 1775, for an army of 170,000 men there
were 60,000 officers—an officer for every three men!
Many of these were of high rank, colonels or generals.

There were so many of them that commands had to be rotated every few months. Most of the officers rarely worked, but they never forgot to draw their pay. Officers' salaries accounted for half of the entire French army budget!

The British army did not have such a top-heavy setup but it had equally bad shortcomings. In a sort of hangover from feudal times, the colonel of each regiment was regarded as an independent contractor; he was paid a certain sum by the War Office, and in return was expected to furnish a trained, equipped regiment. This might have worked if all the colonels had been honest, intelligent men, but many weren't. It was the rule, rather than the exception, for colonels to rake in large sums by methods which were not far from outright stealing. A colonel would report, for instance, 500 men on the regimental roll and draw money for them, when actually there would be 300. The colonel pocketed the difference. Or he would draw 500 pounds sterling to pay for food, contract with a purveyor to feed his regiment for 300 pounds—and the rest was his profit. There were dozens of ways by which a colonel could turn his rank into a very nice business.

The kings, princes, and dukes of the German states looked on their soldiers very much as they looked on their prize cattle. Their armies were made up mostly of young peasants, pressed into service. The rulers quite literally sold their soldiers to foreign powers as mercenaries, getting much of their revenue that way. In 1687 the king of Hesse sold 1,000 men to Venice to fight the Turks. This was the same Hesse which sold troops to King George III of England to fight the American revolutionists—the hated Hessians.

King Frederick William I of Prussia, the father of
Frederick the Great, seems to have regarded his soldiers
as a kind of private zoo. His pets were his royal guard,
the *Lange Kerle*—"Big Guys." During his reign (1713–
40) he spent a total of two years' income from his entire
kingdom buying Lange Kerle, who had to be at least six
feet tall and preferably taller. Frederick William offered
a standing price of 1,000 thaler for a 6-footer and paid
9,000 thaler for an Irishman said to be 7 feet tall. There
were countless stories of the king's agents kidnaping tall
Prussians and making guardsmen out of them, and Prussian parents are said to have hidden sons who were taller
than ordinary. Even a priest was once kidnaped and
made into a royal guard!

The life of a soldier in the 18th century was hard, poor,
and largely without honor. It was also likely to be short.
If he survived his enlistment, or was discharged for dis-
ability, his chances of getting any kind of a pension were
remote indeed. There were a few old soldiers' homes set
up by governments or endowed by public-spirited
citizens. But there weren't nearly enough of them, and
it took the influence of some officer or patron to get into
one. The streets of European cities were full of crippled
soldiers, begging for bread.

It was too bad, of course, and some people tried to
help. But not many had the time to worry about old
soldiers. They had brought their troubles on themselves
by enlisting, hadn't they? Besides, there were so many
more interesting things to think about, in that age of
enlightenment.

CHAPTER II

The Nation in Arms

If you are going to play a game, it's important that everyone knows the rules and promises to stick to them. War is anything but a game, but the same thing holds true: to fight a war by the rule book works only as long as both sides use the same book. If one side ignores it, it may win or it may lose; but whatever happens, the opponents are going to get a shock.

Take one familiar example. England was at war with France in one of those formal conflicts of the 18th century, and the fighting spread to North America. The British sent Major General Edward Braddock 300 miles through the North American wilderness to capture a French fort at the forks of the Ohio.

Braddock was a good general by European rule-book standards, and among his 1,460 men were some of the best troops in the British army. But he failed to grasp that fighting in the forests of the New World required a very different approach. His men marched in their red coats, with flags flying and fifes squealing, probably frightening the bears and raccoons. Near the forks (now

151

Pittsburgh) they were met by a small force of French and Indians, who fought in good Indian style: from behind trees or rocks, dashing in to fire and hiding to reload.

Braddock flatly refused to let his men follow this excellent example. His officers drove the men at sword-point to stay in ranks, loading and firing by command at an enemy they could not see. Of the 1,460 men with Braddock, 456 were killed and 421 wounded. Not one officer escaped unwounded, and Braddock himself suffered a mortal injury. The battle was a stinging, humiliating defeat for the British.

Twenty years later, American militiamen gave the British much the same sort of treatment on the long road between Concord and Boston. A British lieutenant complained: "Our men had very few opportunities of getting good shots at the rebels, as they hardly ever fired but under cover of a stone wall, from behind a tree, or out of a house, and the moment they had fired, they lay down out of sight until they had loaded again or the column had passed."

The British were up against something new in their experience; they were fighting not another army very much like their own, but simply a horde of untrained men.

The rebels broke the rules because they didn't know them; they probably didn't even know that there *were* rules. They had not drilled for hours under the lash of a sergeant's tongue, or been subjected to harsh discipline.

Not that these amateur soldiers always emerged victorious. When the militia met British troops in a regular battle, the professionals generally won. Sometimes the untrained civilian soldiers did a magnificent job, as on the ill-fated expedition to Canada (1775) commanded by Benedict Arnold; the expedition failed but the men, or most of them, conducted themselves like heroes. On other occasions, though, such as the battle of Camden (1780), they disgraced themselves, running in panic without putting up even a show of fight. Eventually the Americans developed professionals of their own, the "Continental Line," who gave a good account of themselves.

Many factors led to the American victory in the Revolutionary War, one of the most important being the help of the French, especially the French navy. What really freed the colonies, though, was the fact that the civilian population fought side by side with the American army against the professional British soldiers.

This wasn't in the rule book at all. The civilian population, as King Frederick had said, wasn't even supposed to know that a war was being fought. But the American civilians organized themselves into guerrilla bands, invaded British camps at night and set fire to supply wagons; they made hit-and-run attacks to free prisoners, chopped down trees to block roads, and destroyed enemy supply trains.

When General John Burgoyne invaded New York from Canada in 1777, the whole countryside rose almost en masse to halt him. By the time he finally reached Saratoga, his 8,000 or so regulars—fine troops, most of them—were confronted with an estimated 20,000 Americans, who had swarmed out from their towns and farms to "stop Burgoyne." Most of them were citizen-soldiers—untrained, poorly disciplined, poorly officered. Nonetheless they overwhelmed Burgoyne by sheer weight of numbers and won a battle which proved to be the turning point of the Revolution.

Two years later General Cornwallis, campaigning in the Carolinas, defeated one force after another of militia, yet never succeeded in subduing the people. The country remained as stubbornly rebel as ever; Cornwallis' army was only a little island in an unfriendly sea, and the island was finally swallowed up at Yorktown.

This nation-in-arms idea—every man a soldier—was not a new one. As we have seen, it dated back to the tribal warfare of ancient times. But it was new to the 18th century, and it meant that the military pattern of small professional armies fighting other small professional armies was on its way out.

The next nation to rise in arms was France, where a long overdue revolution exploded, inspired at least in part by the example of the American colonists. In a grisly poem Sidney Lanier, the American poet, likened the French peasantry to a beaten cur:

"The hound was cuffed, the hound was kicked,
O' the tail was cropped, o' the ears was nicked . . ."

Finally the hound rebelled, leaped into the master's bedroom, and "tore his head from neck to floor, and rolled the head to the kennel door." Exactly that happened in the Reign of Terror, and heads, including those of King Louis XVI and his queen, rolled.

The rulers of the other old settled kingdoms of Europe were alarmed. The French Revolution set a bad example to their own browbeaten subjects, and the rulers of Germany and Austria decided they would have to teach the rebellious Frenchmen a lesson before the situation got out of hand.

Instead, they learned one. A huge army of over 100,000

Germans and Austrians was turned back at the battle of Valmy by a greatly outnumbered French army. It was a strange battle, in which the infantry of the two sides never met; the actual fighting was done by artillery and some cavalry. The French army was an odd collection of royalists and republicans, old-line regiments and untrained volunteers, professional officers and political appointees. By all the rule-book standards, the Germans should have beaten them—but they didn't.

After Valmy, a strong feeling of patriotism swept over the whole French nation. As one historian said, "The fact that the French were not defeated made the battle a victory for them." For hundreds of years, the ordinary Frenchman had taken it for granted that the country belonged to the dukes, marquises, and viscounts. Now, for the first time, the common people felt that the country was theirs and that they, the people, ruled it.

This new patriotic fervor was so intoxicating that France, still in the storm of revolution, sent its hastily reorganized armies tumbling into the Low Countries to bring the same blessings of liberty to its neighbors.

It was an ill-advised crusade and it failed, but it had one far-reaching result. The French revolutionary government, convinced—with justification—that its enemies were just waiting to pounce, set up what amounted to a military dictatorship by committee. The committee speedily announced national mobilization, and decreed that the government had power to requisition anything it needed to supply the armed forces. In short, it ordered the whole nation to take up arms.

In spite of the revolutionary turmoil and years of poor financial management, France was still the richest and potentially the most powerful country in Europe. Hundreds of thousands of young men flocked into the army, all eager to spread the gospel of liberty, equality, fraternity.

It was a completely new kind of an army and for a time it overwhelmed the professional armies of the enemy monarchs.

Compare a typical soldier of the Austrian, Prussian, or British army with a typical soldier of the young French revolutionary army and see the difference:

The first—call him Private Hans Holzkopf—belongs to a despised profession. He became a soldier for no very noble reason: to keep from starving, or because he was in trouble, or—in the case of many Germans and Austrians —because the baron on whose lands he lived had sent around press gangs to round up likely peasants. Hans has gone through a pitiless training, during which certain rules have been pounded into him: Don't think, just obey orders. Don't ask questions; it's none of your business, and besides you're too stupid to understand. He has learned, also, not to draw attention to himself, because that's a sure way of inviting trouble.

Hans is not imaginative and has learned to accept the brutality and harshness of his life if not meekly, at least stoically. He has no great understanding of and no particular interest in the causes or aims of the war in which he happens to be fighting. He is brave only because he has had drilled into him the frightful things that happen to a soldier who runs away or disobeys orders. Hans may lack imagination, but still he knows fear each time he has to stand woodenly in the face of cannon fire.

On the other hand, he is an excellent workman with his musket. Constant drill has enabled him to load and fire it at the rate of four shots a minute—not quite up to the infantrymen of Frederick the Great and their five shots a minute, but very good for a muzzle-loading flint-lock. He is trained to the point where he can go through complicated maneuvers, under fire, in alignment and good order. He is steady and reliable, not likely to break and flee. He has absorbed some esprit de corps, is conscious of a certain pride in his regiment, and keeps his equipment and uniform in good condition.

Look now at his opposite number, Jacques Bon-homme, eighteen years old, until recently a weaver's apprentice in a small French city. Jacques has joined the army because it is the thing to do; all his friends are enlisting. Their families, together with the citizens of their town and members of the weaver's guild, have sent the recruits off in a great outburst of patriotic pride. Jacques is burning with the same pride. It seems a wonderful thing to him that he is no longer a "subject," but a "citizen," and he and his comrades dream of the day when all mankind will be as free as they are. Eagerly they discuss political matters; those who cannot read listen as those who can read aloud from the countless newspapers, tracts, pamphlets, and broadsides which are distributed by the French political parties. The officers join in these talks. There is no great gulf between the officers and the privates, and Jacques addresses his company commander as "Citizen Captain."

The citizen-captain is a young man of Lille, formerly a lawyer, who takes great pleasure in lecturing his company at every opportunity on the glories of France, the wonder of the Revolution, and the evils of their enemies, who are sworn to enslave them again.

Jacques is patriotic where Hans is indifferent; eager where Hans is stolid; and well informed (although in a one-sided way) where Hans is ignorant.

Jacques' military training has been extremely sketchy, however. He knows how to load and fire his musket, but has had hardly any chance to shoot it. His company can perform elementary parade-ground drill, and routine maneuvers, but in a slapdash style that hardly makes up in enthusiasm what it lacks in polish. The officers are an oddly assorted lot. The regimental colonel is a profes-

sional, a holdover from the old regime; but the lawyer-captain knows only what military lore he has been able to absorb by reading and has never glimpsed an enemy.

The French uniforms present an equally odd appearance. Theoretically all the soldiers are supposed to wear blue coats, long white trousers (knee breeches have been rejected because they symbolize the fallen monarchy), and black cocked hats with a tricolor cockade. But the cockade is the only item of the uniform which everybody possesses. Although factories are busy and the women of France have been exhorted to make uniforms, so many men have been called up, and on such short notice, that the suppliers have fallen sadly behind. The officers are lenient about personal appearance, however, and say not a word about unshaven chins, mud-spattered clothes or torn coats.

Jacques looks forward eagerly to battle, when he and his brave citizen-comrades will be able to show the world how the men of free France can fight. He knows nothing whatever about a battle; he has read about them, of course, but has never heard a gun fired except on the drillground, and that not often. He cannot conceive of the stomach-tightening fear that makes a man's breath catch in his throat and sweat pour down his face. He does not know what it means to stand in ranks under fire while his friends are blown into fragments by cannon-balls; or to see some stranger running straight toward him, bayonet extended.

Hans knows all this. Jacques does not; but he will learn.

What happened, then, when the professional met the amateur? If the meeting had been according to the rules, there could have been but one outcome. But like the Americans, the French paid no attention to the rules.

The army in which Hans was a private soldier met the army in which Jacques was a private soldier on a sunny August day in 1794.

Hans's army maneuvered and deployed and formed into line of battle with the same old stately, slow precision. Hans stood rigidly, as he had been taught, in the second rank, his musket loaded and held across his chest, his left foot advanced, his eyes straight ahead.

He heard a strange hullaballoo in front of him. Muskets began to fire. They were in the hands of French skirmishers, men who ran stooping, knelt to fire, stayed down to reload, then ran forward again. This was something new. Some of the men in front of Hans fell; others —Hans among them—stepped forward to fill their places, knowing better than to look down at the bodies writhing at their feet. Then something occurred which was entirely outside Hans's experience—and outside the experience of his officers as well. Behind the skirmishers came a whole army of Frenchmen. Not in order, not in ranks, but simply running forward in a mob—uniforms mostly in rags, many shoeless, some, as Hans's eyes told him, carrying homemade pikes instead of muskets.

He went through the familiar action of presenting his piece and firing. When the smoke lifted, the wave of running Frenchmen was still advancing, and much nearer now. There seemed to be as many of them as ever. They had simply jumped over their dead and wounded.

Hans dropped back to the second rank while he automatically reloaded. The second volley roared out. More Frenchmen fell—but the wave did not stop, did not even slow down. Hans stepped forward, and on command presented his piece once more—

Then he was knocked down, thrown aside like a rag doll, kicked and trampled and destroyed by the wave.

To win that kind of victory required huge masses of men, which the French had. It required also a tremendous enthusiasm, self-confidence, and spirit; these the French had as well. Their armies did not fetter themselves to the old "depot" idea, which required that the army never get far from its supply bases. They did not worry about camp kitchens, or all the cumbersome equipment the professional armies had felt necessary. They did not burden their soldiers with nuisances like powder for the hair, or machines for shaping hats, or polish to shine buttons and shoes.

The French soldiers carried a blanket, perhaps; some extra ammunition, a canteen of water, maybe some hard bread or sausage to eat, and that was all. Traveling so light, they were able to march with dazzling speed, at their revolutionary pace of 120 steps to the minute. They slept where they could, and did not object to unrolling their blankets in a field. True, the passage of a French army was harder on civilians than the passage of an army which brought its own food; no fowl, or pig, or cow, no store of vegetables or fruit or flour lasted long when the French army passed.

Intoxicated by success, still in turmoil at home, the French people made the mistake of turning over their government to a man who seems to have been born for the sole purpose of becoming a military dictator: Napoleon Bonaparte.

He took the magnificent, though unpolished, military machine which the Revolution had bequeathed to him and transformed it into an instrument of tyranny. Under Napoleon, discipline and order came back; not the old brutal discipline which regarded a soldier as an animal rather less important than a cavalry horse, but strict nonetheless. He took the best aspects of the old order—training, discipline, knowledge of tactics—and the best of the new—spirit, confidence, dash—and merged them into the greatest army the world had yet seen.

Napoleon was a military genius, but he brought little that was new to battle. Instead, he utilized all the existing military science of the period, coordinated it, perfected it, and made it bring him victories. He had begun his military career as an artillery officer and knew how best to use the big guns, massing them to blow holes in enemy lines so his cavalry or infantry could break through. He tamed the wild charge of the revolutionaries into a less impetuous but equally effective assault by column. He adopted a battle formation similar to the one used centuries earlier by archers and pikemen: the so-called "mixed order," which alternated columns for assault with a line formation for fire power.

Napoleon posed before the nations of Europe as the great liberator, the man who would free them from age-old servitude. To the French, he constantly stressed the terrible danger they were in from fierce enemies, and how only he, Napoleon, could save them. But after a time even the most gullible Prussian or Austrian whom he had "freed" realized that Napoleon was not a liberator but an enslaver; and the French themselves began to wonder about the terrible price they were paying for "glory."

Napoleon boasted that he could afford to lose 30,000 men a month in his battles. That meant that he was willing that 1,000 soldiers a day, more than 40 every hour, should be sacrificed to his schemes.

He used the powers which had been set up for the revolutionary military dictatorship to keep squeezing more men, more material, more money out of France. During the years he was emperor (he had himself crowned in 1805 and was defeated in 1814) Napoleon called up more than three million men to the army. His armies were by far the biggest that had ever been seen in Europe. In the terrible failure of his invasion of Russia in 1812, nearly half a million soldiers in the French army perished; not all were Frenchmen, by any means, because Napoleon filled up his ranks with conscripts from the nations he conquered.

What Napoleon did, in effect, was to carry the thought of the nation-in-arms to its conclusion. He used the whole might and resources of wealthy France to form and maintain an army. But in doing it, he bled France nearly dry.

Near the end of his career the soldiers in his army were as different from the fervent revolutionaries of 1795 as the revolutionaries were from the professional armies of 1770.

They were mostly conscripts, and not willing conscripts, either. Some still kept the old revolutionary spirit, but the great majority went into the army only because they had no choice. They were likely to be either boys or middle-aged men—the best of the nation's young men had been used up in years of ceaseless bloody wars. Their uniforms were cheap and poor; so were their weapons.

Of course Napoleon's enemies realized very early in their wars with him that it was hopeless to defeat him by sticking to their old ways. They answered conscription with conscription, bending the whole force of their nations to war, as Napoleon had bent the whole force of his.

Napoleon was finally defeated at Waterloo, in 1815, by the British and Prussians. But it had already become obvious to Europe that he was all but finished after the "Battle of the Nations" at Leipzig in August, 1813. For that one battle Napoleon had concentrated more than 300,000 men, and his enemies—Germans, Austrians, Russians, and Swedes—had mustered even more! Compare that with the numbers of men engaged in major battles only a half-century earlier: at Fontenoy fewer than 100,000 on both sides; at Zorndorf, fewer than 80,000.

The French Revolution, and the man who had taken that great movement and used it for his own ends, had changed warfare and changed the kind of man who fought. War was no longer an exercise in politics, to be fought by a small group of professionals. Now whole nations took part in a war and every man was either a soldier or contributed in some way toward keeping the soldier in the field. This was a concept which would have been utterly strange to the men who fought at Fontenoy. It was not new, though. The old Byzantines would have understood.

CHAPTER 12

"Tommy, Fall Be'ind!"

For the first fifteen years of the 19th century, when Napoleon was in his glory and all Europe was at war, it was an honorable thing to be a soldier. Responsibility for the defense of his country rested upon the soldier, and he was both respected and admired.

Then Napoleon was defeated in 1815, shipped off to die on his "lone, barren isle" of St. Helena—and suddenly the attitude toward soldiers changed. People were sick and tired of war, as indeed they had every right to be. They no longer wanted to hear about battles and blockades, sieges, and gallant actions. Their chief desire was to take up their long-interrupted personal lives in peace. Almost overnight the soldier tumbled in public esteem.

The nations on the Continent did not, however, give up the idea of conscription. Prussia, Austria, France, Russia, and other countries were all jealous and fearful of their neighbors, and felt obliged to maintain standing armies. The term of conscription was usually only three years, which young men endured as an unpleasant duty. They looked down on the professional soldiers who formed the cadre of the army, and generally carried their dislike throughout life.

England still distrusted conscription. After Waterloo, she slashed her armies from 685,000 to 100,000, and in effect went back to the old concept of a small, highly trained, long-service professional army.

The soldier was no longer the heroic savior of his country, but merely a young man who had been unlucky enough to get drafted. If he was a career soldier, people assumed he had taken up arms because he couldn't find a more respectable occupation. Once more a gulf opened up between soldier and civilian.

It wasn't quite as wide as it had been a century before. There were always the conscripts, going off reluctantly and coming back joyfully. But the soldier was not a part of ordinary life, as he had been when Napoleon was on the march. He was either tucked away in a barracks, or else—in the case of colony-hunting nations like England and France—off in some remote corner of the earth.

The soldier of 1630 was likely to be regarded with horror; the soldier of 1730 with dislike. The professional career soldier of 1830—when he was thought about at all—was looked on with a sort of amused condescension. In the public eye he had been promoted from the status of a jailbird to that of a ne'er-do-well.

Soldiers were not hated, or even really disliked. But they were felt to be creatures of a coarser fiber than the rest of the population, men who didn't mind hardship, deprivation, and monotony. The general idea of a soldier was of a low-grade character, useful enough in his way —after all, somebody had to do what he did—but hardly the kind of person to invite to one's home. Always excepting the officer corps. All over Europe, army officers were still drawn from the old, aristocratic, land-owning class, the survivors of the feudal system. To a large degree this was true even in democratic America.

Men in the ranks were caricatured as shiftless, lazy, simple-minded, addicted to drink, unable to take care of themselves if someone weren't there to tell them what to do. Writers and cartoonists amused themselves with drawing such portraits of soldiers. The picture was vastly overdrawn. But, in all fairness, it should be said that there was some justice in such a point of view.

The 19th century, for the United States and for most of Europe, was a time of tremendous progress and great opportunity. Why would anybody accept the hazards of army life if he could find something better to do? Why would any intelligent, ambitious man, or any man of reasonable good sense, voluntarily sign up for the tiny pay, the rigid discipline, the isolation, and the scant opportunity that the military life offered?

A few did, of course. These were the adventurers, the restless souls, the ones who always feel the lure of the greener grass in the other field, the young men who yearn for thrills and excitement. There were these in every army, and they provided the leaders in the ranks, the sergeants and corporals who kept armies going. From this kind of man, unfortunately, also come the troublemakers.

The adventurers, though, were far, far outnumbered by the misfits and the unfortunates. Some were driven into the army by sheer poverty. After the terrible Irish famine of 1847–48, for instance, thousands of young

Irishmen could be found in the armies of many of the nations of Europe—most of them in the British army— and in the army of the United States. A bad depression brought hordes of youths anxious to sign up; good times meant lean pickings for the recruiting sergeants.

Many men joined up in rebellion against a monotonous job in mill or mine, hoping, usually in vain, that they would find a better life in uniform. Others were simply drifters, the kind of young man who can't hold a job and wanders from one thing to another until he winds up in military service. There is a fairly common type of person who cannot accept responsibility, but can do a good job if he is told what to do and how to do it, and is content to obey. This type furnished many soldiers.

As a general thing the dullards greatly outnumbered the bright ones; the lazy outnumbered the diligent; and, as always, the followers far outnumbered the leaders. Taken on an average, the professional soldiers of the empire-building 19th century were crude, hard-bitten, tough, and not especially intelligent.

Nonetheless they were good soldiers. They fought in the several great wars which racked the "peaceful" 19th century. When no large-scale wars were being fought—and there weren't nearly as many as there had been in the 18th century—they were fighting to extend the colonial empires of their countries.

Nowadays the words "empire" and "imperialism" have unpleasant connotations. We think of an empire in terms of one people enslaving another, keeping them in bondage by military power and making them work for the benefit of the conqueror. There is a great deal of truth to that concept, but the men who built the empires were proud of what they were doing. They thought of themselves as benefactors, not oppressors, bringing the blessings of civilization to backward and uncivilized peoples.

Most of the wars for colonies were hardly wars at all, although they are usually dignified by the name—the Afghan War, the Zulu War, and so on. They were really expeditions sent out by colonizing nations against backward peoples, to gain territory or commercial advantages.

The people at home liked to read about those "wars," and there were thousands of stories written about fighting in India, or Burma, or Africa. They are fine, full-blooded stories, full of ambushes and sieges, daring escapes, heroic battles, and tragic last stands. Such exciting things did often happen in the course of "pacifying" a colony. But, like the stories about dueling, the tales of the colonial wars give a one-sided picture of reality.

Colonial soldiering, like most other soldiering, consisted of a year of tedium for every day of adventure. A strange exotic land is exciting for a month, perhaps; after that it is familiar and dull, and the climate is usually much worse than the climate at home. Life falls into a monotonous routine. Mysterious diseases claim far more lives than does the enemy. Many soldiers fall victim to that mental affliction the French call *cafard*—which literally means cockroach, but signifies the insanity brought on by isolation, hardship, monotony, and loneliness.

In such a situation, action is welcome as a relief from tedium, although it usually brings considerably increased danger. Rarely is the action a full-scale battle. More often it involves a fruitless chase through jungle or over the desert, with the ever-present chance of ambush or a sudden attack, and torture for those who are captured.

Colonial soldiers lived in a small world whose boundaries were their regiment or even their company. They were usually fiercely loyal to their own group, tolerant of other soldiers, and resentful and contemptuous of civilians. Good soldiers they may have been, but not, necessarily, kindly, patient, or unselfish men. Instead, they were far more likely to be short-tempered, rebellious, and quarrelsome.

Discipline was strict and punishments were severe. In the early years of the 19th century, flogging of soldiers for trivial offenses was universal practice. The custom died out gradually, although it was not abolished in the United States army until 1861, and in the British army not until 1875. Even late in the century, commanders in remote frontier posts could order such drastic punishments as stringing up soldiers by the wrists, spread-eagling them tied by wrists and ankles, or shutting them up in tiny airless sweat-boxes.

The besetting sin of all such colonial armies was drunkenness. In the American frontier army after the Civil War, more than 40 soldiers in every 1,000 underwent treatment for alcoholism—a figure many times higher than the figure for civilians. The same thing was true in the armies of other countries, and the vice afflicted officers as well as enlisted men. Another common failing was gambling; soldiers often lost all their pay only hours after getting it, in games of cards or dice.

On behalf of the soldier it should be said that his harsh, dull life gave him some excuse for drinking and gambling. When soldiers were not on duty there was often quite literally nothing at all for them to do. High army officials considered it none of their business what a soldier did in his free time as long as he didn't get into trouble—but they provided no facilities to help him keep out of trouble. There were no organizations devoted to aiding soldiers, like the Red Cross or USO today. Near most camps there were only privately owned canteens or saloons, whose owners were primarily interested in making money.

A few officers did try to relieve the crushing dullness of garrison life by organizing sports, or study groups, or amateur theatricals. For every one who made the effort, though, there were dozens who thought that such things were beneath their dignity. In general, the soldiers were left to themselves. People at home heard tales of soldiers getting drunk and gambling, and held up their hands in horror, but it rarely occurred to them to do anything about it.

One of the few large-scale wars of the century did help the cause of the common soldier, although it accomplished little else. This was the Crimean War (1854–56) which has the dubious distinction of being one of the most senseless and worst-managed wars ever fought. The combatants were Russia on one side and an odd alliance of England, France, Turkey, and the little kingdom of Sardinia on the other, and the action took place mostly on the Crimean Peninsula of southern Russia. One of the famed encounters of the war was the "Charge of the Light Brigade," a hopeless attack by cavalry on artillery positions. It made a fine poem, but was a piece of bungling typical of the entire conflict.

The incompetence of the commanders on both sides

surpasses belief. Most of them were old men, who had forgotten much and learned little since the Napoleonic Wars—the English commander-in-chief, for example, always referred to the Russian enemy as "the French."

The British planned an ambitious naval attack, designed to pinch off the Crimean peninsula at its narrowest part. To do this, the naval vessels would have to come up close to the shore and open fire with their big guns. It sounded like a good idea and the commanders began to put the plan into effect. Only then did they discover that the water where the attack was planned was only two or three feet deep, and the ships couldn't get anywhere near the shore.

During the siege of Sebastopol, the great Crimean port, a Russian army marched all day long, relying on the only maps they had. They marched in a full circle, and wound up in exactly the same place where they had started!

The misery of the British soldiers was terrible. Some had been sent out to face a Russian winter in summer uniforms, without overcoats. There was no adequate supply system and the armies nearly starved. Worst of all was the plight of the sick and wounded; at one time more than half the British army was unfit for action.

It was left to civilians to reveal the dreadful conditions. The famous Florence Nightingale went to the Crimea to nurse wounded soldiers, an unheard-of thing for a woman to do. She brought back tales of neglect, dirt, lack of elementary care, and the ignorance and incompetence of army doctors.

William Howard Russell of the London *Times*, one of the first war correspondents, telegraphed back stories

which revealed the same shortcomings. Russell got into trouble; the generals were indignant that their bungling had been revealed, and regarded Russell almost as a traitor.

When the sick and wounded began to arrive in England, the great novelist Charles Dickens—one of the writers who had poked fun at soldiers earlier—was horrified by their condition. He wrote a number of articles condemning army callousness and brutality, and other writers and journalists followed suit.

As a result of these exposures the public conscience was finally aroused. Soldiers began to be treated a little

more like human beings and a little less like expendable
animals. But it was a slow process. Almost seventy-five
years after Waterloo, the English poet Rudyard Kipling
could still write protests over the way soldiers were regarded by the rest of the country. His immensely popular
songs and stories of soldier life in India did much to
alter that smug attitude. One of his most effective poems
was "Tommy":

> "I went into a public-'ouse to get a pint o' beer,
>   The publican 'e up an' sez, 'We want no
>   redcoats 'ere . . .'
>   Oh, it's Tommy this, an' Tommy that, an'
>   Tommy, fall be'ind,
>   But it's 'Please to walk in front, sir,' when
>   there's trouble in the wind . . ."

We have spoken of the 19th century after the fall of
Napoleon as being largely a peaceful one. So it was; but
peace is a relative term. There were the incessant colonial
wars and numerous wars of independence. The Greeks
won their freedom from the decaying Turkish Empire,
and so did Serbia and other Balkan nations. The Latin
American countries rebelled against Spain and set up
their own governments. The Italian states turned against
the Austrian Empire and succeeded finally in establish-
ing the nation of Italy. When the century was nearly
three quarters over, the ambition of the German states
to unify themselves led to several conflicts, terminating
in a bloody war between Prussia and France. That war
foreshadowed the titanic struggle which would be known
as the World War.

But the majority of these wars were brief and limited in scope. They could not be compared with the vast upheavals of the Napoleonic age; and they were fought mostly by professional soldiers.

Only one war in the period revived the nation-in-arms idea. This was by far the mightiest conflict of the century, the American Civil War of 1861-65.

Few soldiers on either side were professionals. Before the war the American army had been a good one, but small. Fourteen years earlier it had fought a short, bitter war with Mexico, but that conflict had in no way prepared the nation for the grim struggle which broke out in 1861.

Once more the call went out for huge armies of amateur soldiers. The Union called up 3,375,000 men; the far less populous Confederacy nearly 1,000,000. Again a whole nation was in arms.

CHAPTER 13

On Dress Parade

Soldiers who fought in the wars of Napoleon were birds of gaudy plumage. Even ordinary soldiers of line regiments dazzled the beholder with bright colors, buttons, braid, and sometimes feathers.

In contrast, the soldier of the American Civil War, a half century later, was a sober spectacle. Union infantry wore blue coats and lighter blue trousers, plus a little "forage cap," or *kepi*. Cavalry wore shell jackets, short coats bobbed off at the waist, and tucked their yellow-striped trousers into boots.

Confederate soldiers wore whatever they could find. It wasn't uncommon to see whole companies of Rebs decked out in Union blue, the result of a raid on a Union supply train. Some Confederate officers wore elegant tailored uniforms of gray—at least in the early part of the war—but only a few of the rank and file ever owned complete uniforms. Most of the Southern soldiers had only homespun and home-dyed trousers and jackets of "butternut," a neutral color which was as much yellow and brown as it was gray.

176

Military uniforms, as we think of them today, are only a few centuries old. They were adopted by armies on a widespread scale, reached heights of gorgeousness, and faded back into drabness, all within a comparatively short time.

But in a broader sense, military uniforms are older than soldiers. The war paint and scalp lock of an Indian warrior was a uniform in that sense; they marked him as a fighting man. No doubt cave dwellers, gathering for a raid, daubed themselves with paint to frighten their enemies, and wore a headdress of wolf or bear skin to borrow, magically, the fighting qualities of those animals. But these were not true uniforms.

It might be argued that armor was a uniform, in that it proclaimed its wearer as a fighting man; but armor is protection, not a uniform. Two centuries before Christ certain regiments of Hannibal's Carthaginian armies wore special tunics of blue or green, which were true uniforms. From time to time in later periods, some companies or regiments all dressed alike. But for most of man's long history, a soldier could be distinguished from a civilian only by the fact that he carried weapons.

In the Middle Ages, it was customary for great lords to have their followers wear the lord's *blazon,* or coat of arms, to show who their leader was. This might be regarded as a uniform, but it could be an unreliable guide in the melee of a medieval battle. Think of coming up against a man swinging an axe and wearing a livery of a black eagle on a red background. You wouldn't have much time to figure out which lord displayed that blazon, and whether he was on your side or the enemy's. Besides, each lord displayed his arms as seemed best to him, and many didn't bother to outfit their followers at all.

Through history, it was common practice for all the men in one army to bear some distinguishing mark, so they could tell friend from foe. The mark might be a white cloth around the arm, or a sprig of holly or some other plant in the hat. The drawbacks to this makeshift system are obvious. Suppose you lost your white cloth, or the holly fell out of your hat? And all an enemy had to do to disguise himself was to put holly in his own hat.

In the later Middle Ages, the free companies affected a sort of uniform which merely said, "Look out! I'm a soldier!" Their uniform consisted of an exaggerated version of civilian clothes, which in that period were exaggerated enough themselves. If baggy breeches were fashionable, a pikeman or arquebusier strutted around in breeches so baggy he had to walk spraddle-legged. When it was modish to wear a plume in the hat, the soldier sported three or four. When styles called for men to wear slashed and puffed sleeves and trunk hose, mercenary soldiers wore sleeves, doublets, and trunk hose so puffed and slashed that they looked like caricatures. This sort of outfit was characteristic of the German *Landsknechts*, mercenaries of the 15th and 16th centuries, who were good fighters but had a reputation as bullies and robbers. Pictures of Landsknechts make you wonder how anybody could get into such an outfit in the first place, let alone fight in it.

It was only with the beginning of national armies that true uniforms began to appear. Henry VII of England founded the Yeoman Warders of the Tower of London in 1485, and put them into a uniform which remains much the same today. Elizabeth I gave some of her guardsmen a "russet coat," which served as a uniform. Certain French regiments were distinguished by a *tabard,* a sleeveless garment which was hardly more than a length of cloth with a hole in the middle for the head.

The general usually credited with being the first to dress his soldiers in a true national uniform was Oliver Cromwell, the Parliamentary leader of the English Civil War in the middle of the 17th century. Actually the uniform was merely a variation of the civilian dress of the period, much the same sort of clothing the Pilgrim Fathers wore: long coat, loose knee breeches, and a wide felt hat. There was an important difference, though; every soldier's coat was red, and his breeches were gray. One story says that Cromwell outfitted his men in this manner because he got a bargain on huge amounts of red cloth. Regiments were distinguished by the *facings* of various colors which were sewn on their coats. Facings are ornamental strips of cloth. Sometimes the lining of the coat was of a contrasting color, and was displayed by buttoning back the coat skirts or lapels.

The idea of easily distinguished uniforms was such a good one that within a short time most other nations adopted their own. All of the uniforms were designed to be conspicuous and easily seen. In the rule-book battles fought in the 17th and 18th centuries, an eye-catching uniform was a great advantage. A general watching the action could instantly see where his own men were and where the enemy was. There was no need for camouflage. With the feeble range of guns in those days, you had to be almost close enough to the enemy to hit him with a rock before you could hit him with a bullet. A fiery red or shining white coat was no handicap.

There were other reasons why generals hailed the idea of a standard uniform. Desertion was a serious problem, and a man in a gaudy uniform had a much harder time sneaking away than a man whose only uniform was a sprig of holly. Uniforms also allowed standards of neatness to be set and maintained, and proved a definite morale builder. A man in a military uniform has a sense of pride, of unity with his fellows, and an esprit de corps which is priceless in battle.

The uniform of Cromwell's time was copied, with some modification, until the early part of the 18th century. It was a good, sturdy uniform, loose enough to let the soldier move freely and rugged enough to stand hard wear. But fashions changed. Civilian clothes for men got tighter, and uniforms, after a time, followed suit.

The wide-brimmed hat of Cromwell's days was turned up on one side, then on two more, and became the familiar three-cornered hat, the *tricorne*. Soldiers began to wear long gaiters, fastened with many buttons, over their woolen stockings. Coats came to be decorated all over with badges, buttons, buckles, loops, and stripes. The whole uniform lost its loose, comfortable appearance and began to look more "military."

When Harry Jenkins, the London orphan who took the king's shilling near the middle of the 18th century, paraded in full dress uniform, he and his comrades made a dazzling sight. On their black tricornes were blue and white cockades, and their red coats showed blue facings against the shining brass buttons. Their powdered hair hung in a long queue. Their shoes, of course, were black, but the rest of the uniform was a spotless white: the long waistcoat, the cross belts supporting the bayonet and cartridge case, the breeches, and the gaiters.

It took a great deal of Harry's time to keep his uniform looking even respectable, let alone dazzling. The cloth was shoddy, carelessly woven and shabbily dyed. Cloth sold to the army was supposed to pass a rigid inspection, but the inspectors could be bribed easily enough. The red of the coat had a tendency to run and fade, turning the blue facings purple and leaving a faint pink tinge on the breeches. The brass buttons and badges tarnished easily. The shoe leather was almost as stiff and unyielding as wood, and stubbornly resisted efforts to bring it to a polish with soot and tallow. The cocked hat needed eternal brushing, especially when it got wet, which happened regularly in rainy England.

The white cloth of the breeches was so poor that they could be washed only infrequently or they would simply disintegrate. They were kept white by rubbing and brushing in pipe clay, a fine white powder. In rainy weather the pipe clay quickly became a sort of paste, uncomfortable in the extreme. In dry weather, as the soldiers marched, the pipe clay flew up in a cloud. Even so, Harry and his contemporaries took an odd pride in the very discomforts their uniforms caused. No soft civilian could wear such clothes or keep them looking so well!

There were only two parts of the uniform that soldiers of the time wholeheartedly hated. One was the stiff, high, tight leather stock which buckled around the neck. The stock had one advantage: it forced a soldier to keep his head high and his eyes straight ahead. But it had disadvantages as well. French soldiers called their recruits "Blues" because their stocks were so tight that it was

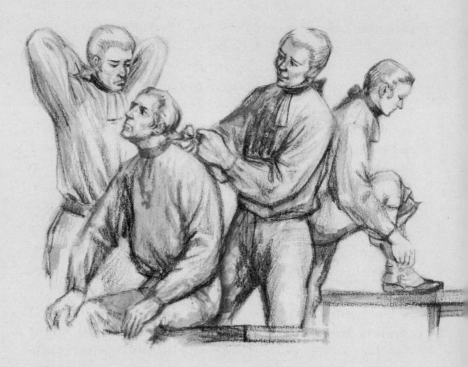

said their faces turned blue from lack of air.

The stock was a minor hardship, though, compared to the powdered hair and the long, stiff queue, required by regulations, that hung down the back of every soldier. Harry longed to became a sergeant if for no other reason than that sergeants wore wigs—hot, heavy, and itchy, maybe, but still much to be preferred to the queue.

Because long hair made a more impressive queue, soldiers let their hair grow until in some cases it hung to their waists. Those with bald spots had an especially hard time of it; they had to fill out their scanty locks with hanks of false hair.

Getting his queue ready to pass inspection was a torture for Harry. First, of course, he combed out his long

hair. (Sometimes he washed it. Not too often, though, because everyone knew such a practice laid a man open to all kinds of chills and rheums.) Then he greased it all over with candle grease, and rubbed in a sort of pomade. After that came the worst part, the braiding or plaiting, and for this Harry needed help. He would plait a friend's hair, and the friend in turn would do Harry's. Colonel

H. de Watteville, in his book *The British Soldier,* says
that unpopular men had a hard time finding a comrade
to help them. They often had to plait their own hair,
usually failed to pass inspection, and had to do it all over
again.

It was a point of pride among sergeants that their men
pull back their hair as hard as possible—so tight that
soldiers said wryly that if they could close their eyes after
the hairdressing operation, it hadn't been done properly.
One regiment was so insistent on tugging the hair back
that it gained the name of the "Hard-and-Tights."

To keep hair pulled back in that painful way, a ring-
like device known as a *rooter* was forced in firmly, while
the victim's eyes watered. Then the hair was gathered
around a curious thing known as a *pad,* a cigar-shaped
bag filled with horsehair or sand, and braided tight. The
operation was finished off with another coat of pomade
and the queue secured with a leather thong. Finally,
powder was dusted over the whole coiffure.

After all that work and discomfort, a soldier didn't dare
get his hair mussed. Many a man sat up all night before
an important inspection rather than risk having to go
through the torture again in the morning. The grease and
pomade which stiffened the hair also attracted bugs,
and stories are even told of soldiers being awakened by
rats nibbling at their hair, lured by the candle grease.

It's hard to see why the armies of the time insisted on
such an idiotic custom as powdered hair and queues.
They did, though, and when the British army finally
abolished it in 1804, there were dark mutterings from
hard-nosed old officers who predicted such looseness
would lead to mutiny. The rest of the army cheered.

As the 18th century drew to a close, European army uniforms kept getting tighter, showier, and more impractical. It was during and shortly after the Napoleonic wars that uniforms reached their height of gorgeousness—and silliness. Looking at pictures of soldiers of that day, you wonder how they were expected to march, let alone fight, in what they had to wear. Some British and French soldiers in those wars must have served in America during the Revolution. They probably wished they were dressed in a sensible fighting outfit like the ones worn by the American riflemen: a loose brownish-gray hunting jacket of deerskin or heavy cloth, leggings, moccasins, and a cap.

The uniforms they actually wore were for the most part preposterous. The jackets were so tight that a man could hardly put one on by himself—he had to be eased into it by a friend. The leather stocks were higher and tighter than ever, and the collar of the jacket was so tall that a man couldn't turn his head. By then they had got rid of the long stockings but the trousers were as tight as the jackets. Soldiers complained that if they sat down carelessly, the trousers split. There were no pockets because they were considered unmilitary.

Worst of all, perhaps, were the hats, which came in an astonishing variety, all uncomfortable. Most soldiers wore a tall *shako*, the "tar bucket," still to be seen on the dress uniform of West Point cadets. Some resembled a leather stovepipe. Others flared out at the top and looked something like a coal scuttle. They gave little protection from sun or rain and must have been miserably hot and heavy.

Most soldiers fought their campaigns in exactly the same uniforms they paraded in at home. The idea of one uniform for dress and one for combat hadn't occurred to anyone yet.

No doubt a French regiment of Napoleon's time looked splendid on parade, with their white belts pipe-clayed, their brass shining, the dye of their jackets fresh and unfaded. But what must the same regiment have looked like after a hard campaign such as Napoleon fought against England in Spain and Portugal? Ragged, faded, shoes in shreds, hats shapeless, buttons missing, brass green with corrosion.

The cavalry went in for spectacular uniforms even more than the infantry did. The cavalry arm of every nation had more or less standardized branches. There were the dragoons, for instance, who were originally mounted infantry; they rode to battle but fought on foot. There were cuirassiers, heavy cavalry who wore *cuirasses*, breastplates, and were descendants of the old armored knights. Besides their breastplates they wore helmets with a crest of feathers or horsehair, heavy jackboots and gauntlets. Lancer regiments were distinguished by their odd-shaped hat, the *czapka*, adopted from Poland; it had a wide, square top which could be pushed in or out like an accordion.

Most gorgeous of all were the hussars, light cavalry who wore uniforms patterned after the Hungarian style, which seemed to consist mostly of braid, buttons, and loops. The hussars carried curved sabers and wore a *busby*, a cylindrical fur hat with a cloth bag hanging from it; glossy boots, skin-tight breeches, and a fur-trimmed overjacket. This overjacket was rarely put on, just hung from one shoulder. Hussar regiments were usually the proudest and most aristocratic in an army.

Such uniforms might have been acceptable when a soldier's main duty was to stand stiffly in ranks, even during battle. But when that kind of battle was no longer fought, the tight, gaudy, uncomfortable uniforms became a hazard as well as a hindrance. Guns were improved, battles were fought at longer range, and the advantages of a less conspicuous uniform became apparent. It finally occurred to the top brass that it was silly to fight a war in costume, and perhaps someone even spared a thought for the men in the ranks.

Armies began issuing field uniforms that were simpler, less expensive, and more comfortable than the old ones, even if they were less showy. Dress uniforms were kept in mothballs for parades, which is where they belonged. Old habits died hard, though. The British wore their red coats into battle for the last time at Khartoum, in 1884. The French hung on even longer. They were still dressing some of their soldiers in red trousers and blue coats in the opening months of World War I, in 1914.

Fashions in uniforms came and went, and often the uniform of a victorious army was copied by other nations. The French kepi—a cap with a flat top and hard bill—became popular after French victories in Algiers in the 1830's. The forage cap of the Union army during the Civil War was modeled after it. When the French were defeated by the Prussians in 1871, many countries, including the United States, put their soldiers into the Prussian spiked helmet.

In our Civil War there appeared some strange apparitions, inspired by the French wars in Algiers. These were the Zouave regiments who wore the uniform of Moorish troops in the French army: baggy trousers, usually red, gaudy sashes, fancy short jackets, and tasseled fezzes. There was a great fad for Zouave regiments, but the uniform was as out of place in the woods of Virginia as it would have been in Greenland. The colorful Zouaves must have taken an unmerciful ribbing from the other soldiers, and it wasn't long before they were outfitted in regular Union blue.

By the close of the last century, most armies were in drab, practical uniforms. The French favored horizon-blue. The British adopted khaki, a muddy color they used first in India; it was supposed to have originated when troops, finding themselves easy targets in white, rolled in mud for camouflage. Italy went in for blue-gray; and Germany and several other countries used *feldgrau*, or field gray.

The United States stuck to blue for a long time, and didn't issue its first khaki uniforms until the Spanish-American War, which began in 1898. American soldiers complained bitterly, though—due to army confusion they wore heavy blue woolen uniforms in the jungles of Cuba, and got the light cotton khaki only when they returned to the United States in late fall.

American uniforms of World War I were ugly in the extreme. Ugliest of all were the spiral puttees—strips of cloth wound around the legs—and the little "overseas cap," whose sole virtue was that it could be folded and put into a pocket.

Modern soldiers have little to complain about in their uniforms. They may not be attractive, but they are scientifically designed for comfort and utility. A soldier today has available a variety of outfits which would completely bewilder a member of the Grand Army of the

Republic, who considered himself lucky if his shoes come close to fitting. Today's private is given clothes designed to be worn in a steaming jungle, or in the killing cold of the Antarctic. He has fatigue uniforms, service uniforms, dress uniforms. His battle dress usually looks like nothing so much as a pair of coveralls.

All his clothes fit, in spite of the old jokes about the quartermaster sergeant asking the recruit, "Do you want it too big or too small?" His hats and shoes are engineered according to medical and scientific advice. He generally has a laundry and even a dry cleaner at his disposal.

Best of all, perhaps, he keeps his hair neat with a barber's clippers. He doesn't have to powder and braid it.

CHAPTER 14

The World at War

The American Civil War was fought with weapons which were outmoded even while they were being manufactured. Within a few years after the fighting ended, they would be museum pieces, not much more useful than arbalests or catapults.

Most of the infantry on both sides was equipped with muzzle-loading, smoothbore muskets, and most of the artillery with muzzle-loading, smoothbore cannon. Better weapons were known; breech-loading rifles were in use, and so were rifled cannon. There was even a primitive kind of machine gun available. In the course of the Civil War some troops were armed with rifles but for a number of reasons, muskets were retained as the mainstay.

The Civil War was the last great conflict fought with muskets. Within a few years of its close the United States, and most of the nations of Europe, had supplied their forces with rifled weapons. The Franco-Prussian War of 1870-71 was fought with rifles.

A rifled gun is one which has spiral grooves inside the barrel. The grooves impart a spin to the projectile and

190

send it farther, faster, and straighter, with less powder.

Besides being rifled, the new weapons were breech-loading instead of muzzle-loading. This increased their rate of fire immensely, and eliminated the old clumsy exercise with a ramrod, which made it all but impossible for a soldier to reload his gun while he was lying down or even kneeling. Instead of black powder, the propelling charge was smokeless powder, which was much more powerful and more stable, and did not give off clouds of choking smoke.

Rifled weapons (we are speaking now of handguns) were not new. They were, in fact, almost as old as smoothbores. As early as the 16th century, the rifle was a favorite hunting weapon in Europe. It didn't find favor as a military weapon, though, because it presented grave problems. For one thing, it was terribly slow to load; the bullet had to be hammered down into the barrel, to fit the grooves. If for some reason the load had to be drawn, it was next to impossible to get the bullet out again. Burnt powder fouled the grooves so badly after firing that the barrel had to be scraped every few rounds.

Since military tactics of the time depended on getting up close to the enemy and firing massive unaimed volleys, range and accuracy weren't nearly as important as rate of fire, and the rifle remained a hunter's gun.

The first war in which the rifle played a significant part was the American Revolution. Corps of riflemen, armed with the long "Kentucky rifle," distinguished themselves as scouts and skirmishers. In the hands of an expert the Kentucky rifle was a fine weapon. Its bullet didn't have to be hammered down. Instead, the bullet was put on an oiled "patch," a round piece of cloth or thin leather, and rammed home. The patch served to engage the grooves and impart the spin. It also prevented much of the bore fouling by acting as a swab, clearing the bore of powder residue from the previous round.

The rifle was still far slower in rate of fire than the musket, though. Only a relatively few gunsmiths made rifles, because a laborious hand process was involved. And a rifleman, like the archer of an earlier day, had to undergo a long apprenticeship before he became a marksman. For these reasons, most of the revolutionary troops still fought with the flintlock musket.

The advantages of the rifle were so obvious, however, that the problem of designing a rapid-firing rifle engaged the attention of many inventors. By the time of the Civil War, the musket was well on its way to becoming an anachronism.

Artillery followed a similar pattern of development. For centuries, fieldpieces had been simple tubes of iron, or sometimes bronze, which fired solid iron balls. Some improvements had been made over the years. A fairly effective explosive projectile had been invented, and designers had found better ways of elevating the muzzle.

Nevertheless, the artillery of the Civil War was basically the same as the artillery of Fontenoy, or even of the Thirty Years' War. The gunners loaded powder and shot by ramming it down the muzzle. They "laid"—aimed—their piece, and fired it through a touchhole in the barrel. The gun went off with an enormous cloud of blinding, stifling smoke as the gun carriage, trail, wheels, and all, slammed back several feet with the recoil. Then came the ritual of wrestling the gun back into position with rope and handspike, and re-laying it between every two rounds.

Within a few years after the Civil War, improvements in artillery came at a startlingly rapid rate. Rifled barrels meant immensely greater range and accuracy. Smokeless powder allowed the gunners to see what they were doing and to watch where the shot fell. Breech-loading replaced the complex swabbing and ramming with a simple tug on a lever. The recoil was absorbed by springs or hydraulic cylinders. Only the gun barrel jumped back; the carriage stayed put and the piece didn't have to be re-laid. New kinds of fuzes on the projectiles could be set to throw a deadly shower of red-hot fragments when they burst.

In the Civil War, 12 rounds an hour with a gun was good shooting. Not many years later, a gun with many times the range and destructive power could fire that many, and often more, *per minute*.

All this meant, obviously, that the kind of battle which was fought at Fontenoy was no longer possible. Advancing in orderly ranks against muskets firing at best four rounds a minute, with an effective range of less than 100 yards, was costly, but it could be done successfully. Even if the enemy was entrenched or protected behind breastworks, as the Americans were at Bunker Hill, the advance could still succeed. In that case, though, the cost in casualties—the "butcher's bill," as the soldiers called it—was all but prohibitive.

Even before muskets gave way to rifles, soldiers were showing themselves extremely reluctant to march in ranks against enemy positions, and good officers were just as reluctant to order them to do so. More and more soldiers were put into the advance line of skirmishers, who ran ahead as individuals, not in a closely packed mass. Dodging and widely separated, they presented a much more

difficult target to the volleys of the defenders. Eventually the fast-moving skirmishers became the only attacking force, running to the attack in waves. The marching ranks of soldiers in close-order formation became as obsolete as the armored knight.

But attacking with waves of running soldiers could be as costly in human lives as the old method. On a large scale, the results of such an attack over open ground were appalling. In one famous instance—General Pickett's charge at Gettysburg—4,800 Confederate troops, with only feeble artillery support, advanced over 1,400 yards of open ground against entrenched Union artillery and infantry. The charge was brave to the point of foolhardiness. The desperate Confederates succeeded at first in crashing through the first line of defense, then broke in the face of a storm of fire. Of the 4,800 men who began the doomed charge, 3,393 were left behind on the field as casualties.

If such a charge against muskets was almost bound to fail, a charge against rapid-fire rifles certainly would. And if the defending riflemen were backed up by quick-firing artillery and machine guns, such a charge would be suicide.

After most armies were equipped with all three weapons, the defense gained a tremendous advantage over the attack. But, in war, someone has to attack, and the problem facing the generals was: How can a defense line be broken? It was a problem which was to plague them for years, and cost, quite literally, millions of lives.

Almost exactly fifty years after the Civil War ended, the generals were provided with a huge, ghastly laboratory in which to test their theories on attack versus defense. It was called World War I.

The war had been a long time in coming. After 1815, when Napoleon fell, the 19th century was for the most part a time of peace, but old jealousies and resentments burned as strongly as ever. The Franco-Prussian War in 1870-71 rekindled the old hatred between the French and the Germans. Austrians hated Italians and Italians hated Austrians. The Russians were bound by sympathy to the Slavic countries of the Balkans, which felt themselves oppressed by the Austro-Hungarian Empire. The Austrians were tied to the Germans. The French and British had a treaty, although neither really trusted or liked the other. The Germans were jealous of British sea power and envied her colonial possessions. All Europe was one vast web of suspicion and intrigue.

Still, the shaky peace held, year after year, in spite of endless "incidents" and threats. As the 19th century drew to a close and the new century began, the nations of the Continent still put their faith in conscription, the universal draft. The system was responsible for untold thousands of young men emigrating to America, where there was no obligatory army service.

England frowned on conscription, trusting instead in her small army of professionals, and most of all in her "senior service," her great navy. The United States still felt itself remote from the quarrels of Europe and relied on its small army, its navy, and basically on the wide Atlantic Ocean, to keep it remote.

Year by year the tensions grew. It was obvious that something had to give, and something finally did. The First World War was actually triggered by the assassination of an Austrian archduke in 1914, but almost any other incident would have done as well.

The quickly growing war pitted the "Allies" against the "Central Powers." The Allies were France, Russia, England, the small countries of Belgium and Serbia, and later Italy; eventually they were joined by a host of other nations, including Japan and the United States. The Central Powers were Germany and Austria-Hungary, joined later by Turkey and Bulgaria.

The time of the nation-in-arms had come again. Nearly every family in the warring nations sent at least one son into the armed forces. Some went gladly and confidently, burning with patriotism, relieved that the long time of waiting had ended at last. Others, more farsighted or less optimistic, went to war with resignation; still others with dread and foreboding. But not even the most pessimistic foresaw the four years of horror which lay ahead. And neither did the leaders of the countries engaged.

The main theater of war was in Europe. On the "Eastern Front," the armies of Germany and Austria met the armies of the Russian Empire—huge, unwieldy, poorly trained and armed, and often incompetently led. The war on the Eastern Front alone was a gigantic conflict of epic proportions, many times greater in scope than any previous war. For all their miserable training and equipment, the brave, patient, loyal Russian peasant-soldiers gave a fine account of themselves. They were eventually defeated, in 1917, and their armies destroyed—whereupon Communism jumped into the vacuum, and raised new problems which still plague us today.

In the Alps, Austria and Italy fought a savage mountain war under conditions of frightful hardship. It was an indecisive, bloody struggle which ended only with the final collapse of the Austro-Hungarian Empire and its partner, Germany. There was also bitter fighting in the Near East, in Africa, and on most of the world's oceans.

When we think of World War I, however, we are most

likely to think of the "Western Front." Here the armies
of Germany slammed head on against the armies of Belgium, France, and England.

Germany had a magnificent army, superbly equipped
and trained. It was commanded by the best generals of
the time, who had been planning the war for years.
France also had a magnificent army—not quite so well
trained, perhaps, or so well equipped, but possessed of
enormous dash and spirit and burning to revenge the
defeat of 1871. The British professional army was by far
the smallest but it was also, man for man, probably the
best.

In August, 1914, following a long-perfected plan, Germany sliced through neutral Belgium and tried to knock
France out of the war. The Germans hoped, and believed, that they would be back home "before the leaves
fall from the trees."

The plan failed. Why it failed is still being argued.
For one thing, the German attack was unexpectedly
slowed by the heroic resistance of the Belgians, the
French, and the British, whose small army was all but
wiped out. And fear of the vast Russian army, moving
like a glacier toward eastern Germany, kept the Germans
from committing as many troops to the Western Front
as originally planned.

For whatever reason, the drive to end the war quickly
in the West was halted. The German advance was
stopped, not very far from Paris. Within weeks, a solid
battle front stretched from the North Sea in Belgium to
the mountains of neutral Switzerland. Along those hundreds of miles, millions of men faced each other, in some
places only a few yards apart.

And there they stayed for four long years.

There had been no war like it in history. The front might be compared to that ancient battle between two groups of bronze age spearmen: masses of men shoving at each other with hardly any movement to be seen.

Like the bronze age warriors, neither side dared retreat, and neither side knew how to advance. Defense was still far superior to attack, but neither army could simply sit and wait to be attacked. Wars are not won that way. Both the Allies and the Central Powers tried to break the enemy lines in the only way they knew—by sending waves of men with rifles to attack, in much the same way that General Pickett had done at Gettysburg.

The results were horrible.

The soldiers moved ahead into an inferno of artillery and machine gun fine, were shot down by the hundreds of thousands, and gained nothing. The deadly guns made the surface of the ground unlivable, so both sides went underground, into trenches.

Trenches were not new, but nothing like these trenches had been seen before. They began as simple ditches in which riflemen crouched, but under the searching, blasting shellfire they got deeper and more complex. The front evolved into a maze of molelike burrowings with first, second, and third line trenches, strong points, advanced and command posts, communicating trenches and dugout shelters. In these trenches men lived for weeks, venturing out only at night to patrol or to bring in wounded.

Among and behind the trenches squatted thousands of pieces of artillery, from deadly little 75's to mammoth howitzers, guns which fired a heavy shell at a high trajectory. The cannon spoke constantly. Between the lines lay "No Man's Land," a desolation of mud, barbed wire, shell holes, mine fields, and corpses.

Generals on both sides talked grandly of breaking the enemy's front. The difficulty was that they had no notion of how to go about it, except to send more thousands of men against the guns. There were no flanks to be turned; one flank rested on the ocean, the other on the Alps. There was no way to maneuver. There was no way to hide massive troop movements.

Attacks fell into a deadly pattern. One side or the other would concentrate hundreds of thousands of men along a few miles of front, hoping to surge ahead and punch a hole in the enemy defenses. But the enemy would invariably find out about the planned attack. How could such a concentration be hidden when the lines were so close together and there were only a few roads or rail lines to bring up materials and men? Spies were active on both sides and scouts in airplanes kept a close watch from the sky.

The attackers would mount a furious artillery barrage, sending over a hailstorm of shells to soften up the defenders. The defenders would hide in their dugouts until the barrage ended. Then they would man the parapets to meet the main attack—infantrymen clutching bayoneted rifles, swarming "over the top" of the trenches and into No Man's Land.

As soon as the infantrymen appeared, the guns of the defenders would open up. The attacking soldiers might overrun two or three outer defense lines, at tragic cost. But the farther they got from their own guns, the closer they got to the big guns of the enemy. They could not be supplied with food or ammunition, and the attack would bog down. The enemy would counterattack; and after days or weeks of frightful fighting, the battle would die down with nothing really changed.

Except that whole armies of men would be dead or wounded.

Even on a quiet sector of the front, with no big battle going on, the armies figured on "wastage" of several thousand men a week. This terrible word meant men killed or wounded on routine patrol or by casual artillery fire; those who died of illness, or accident, or whose nerves gave way under the strain and who had to be sent back with "shell shock." These men were wastage.

Great battles like those at the Somme, the Marne, Verdun, Ypres, and the Argonne killed and mutilated soldiers at a horrifying rate. At the battle of the Somme the attacking British suffered a half million casualties. In that same battle the Germans sent in 66 divisions, of which 44 were mauled so badly that they ceased to exist as units. French losses were so heavy that at one period the army mutinied and there was grave doubt that France could continue the war.

It was largely a war of artillery. Big guns by the thousand rained down shells incessantly. Of the millions of men who were killed or wounded more than half—perhaps as many as three fourths—were victims of artillery fire. Machine guns accounted for a large percentage of the rest. Except in the early days of the war only a comparative few were killed by rifle fire, and fewer by bayonets. Even so, when the command "Over the top!" was given, the infantrymen climbed their ladders and trotted out into the muddy waste of No Man's Land with their rifles and bayonets.

New weapons made their appearance, weapons which the generals hoped would overcome the deadly stalemate and end the war. One was the flame thrower, a device which squirted liquid fire out of a nozzle. The Germans introduced poison gas, sending clouds of choking, burning fumes over the enemy trenches. Gas added a new horror, but it was not a very efficient weapon, actually, and could be guarded against by providing soldiers with gas masks.

The British invented a self-propelled, caterpillar-tread armored vehicle they called a "tank." This might have turned the tide of the war; a tank was impervious to

small-arms fire and could lumber through shell holes where a wheeled vehicle could not go. But the British were too impatient to put their tanks into action, threw too few of them into battle too soon, and gave the Germans time to work up defenses against them.

Airplanes, new to battle, caught the public's fancy. They were invaluable for scouting and reporting enemy troop movements, and did some damage by dropping bombs; but the primitive, vulnerable, and undependable fighters and bombers of 1914-18 did not have a decisive effect on the war. Neither did the huge dirigibles, the Zeppelins, which the Germans used in terror raids on England—a grim foreshadowing of the bombing raids of World War II.

In the end, the heaviest burden of fighting rested on the foot soldier, what the English called the "P.B.I."—the "poor bloody infantry." For soldiers on both sides, the early optimism and high spirits gave way to a sort of sullen, dogged courage. In other wars a battle had lasted a few hours, a day, two or three days at the very most. In World War I battles went on for days, for weeks, sometimes for months.

The trenches became a way of life. Amid the mud, the stench, the dirt, soldiers managed to live and even find a few comforts. When they were relieved from the front lines for a few days (or hours) of rest, the soldiers could sing and laugh, forgetting for a little while the fact that they were going back. They never spoke of someone "getting killed." A soldier "went west," or "caught a packet," or "bought it." It was as if the soldiers hoped that they could somehow avoid death by never mentioning it.

On and on the war dragged, with the generals still trying feverishly to break through the enemy lines, failing every time, paying with thousands of lives for a few yards of muddy shell holes. They kept talking about the big breakthrough, when the enemy's lines would be pierced and the cavalry sent galloping through to mop up.

The cavalry waited four years for the breakthrough—which never came.

In one respect, the division between soldier and civilian was all but erased in World War I; in another respect it was wider than ever. Civilians did not look down on soldiers or dislike them; how could they, when most civilians had a near relative serving in France? Workers felt themselves very much a part of the war, as indeed they were.

Practically all production in the combatant nations went to feeding the war, which was using up material even faster than it was using up soldiers. At the Somme, for instance, the French alone fired more than 12 million artillery shells within a few weeks. But the soldiers felt that no civilian could understand what life in the trenches was like. They reacted with resentment and disgust when some well-paid munitions worker said, "We're all in this together." A British writer and poet, Robert Graves, himself a veteran of the war, said, "A great gulf of heroism and uncommunicable horror separated the trench soldier from the civilian."

The deadlock remained unbroken, through 1915, 1916, 1917, and on into 1918. Finally, even the generals stopped talking about the big breakthrough and began to speak of a "war of attrition"—wearing the enemy down to exhaustion and making him lose his will to fight. There's one big flaw in that theory—it wears your own men down too, and it becomes a question of which side loses its will to fight first.

The soldiers fought on with dull fatalism. They hoped to live through the war but had given up believing they would. They no longer believed in tremendous victories or great breakthroughs, either. They accepted the war as something which always had existed and always would, and felt themselves caught up in an endless nightmare of mud, cold, fear, and despair.

In the end, which came November 11, 1918, the Central Powers were defeated. The defeat was largely due to the strangling sea blockade which prevented Germany from replacing the enormous quantities of raw materials, fuel, and lubricants it used. German efforts to break the blockade by submarine warfare almost, but not quite, succeeded. Entrance of the United States into the war in 1917 pumped fresh hope into the faltering Allies. After one last despairing attack Germany, enfeebled and with a generation of her young men dead, gave up.

Headlines in Allied countries exulted, "We've won!" and cynical soldiers asked, "Won what?"

Out of 65 million men mobilized in all countries in World War I, 37½ million men were casualties. Not all of these were killed, by any means; the word "casualties" includes those dead of disease or accident, the wounded, the prisoners, and the missing. But 8½ million had been killed—a staggering total.

Russia suffered 76 per cent casualties; France, 73 per cent; Austria-Hungary, 90 per cent; Germany, 64 per cent. Stunning as these percentages are, they fail to convey the suffering, the shattered lives, the grief and despair that lay behind the statistics.

After World War I had ended, there was a tremendous revulsion of feeling against war and all it stood for. For once, though, this revulsion did not include the ordinary soldier. People felt, and quite justly, that the soldier was the greatest victim of all. No one—soldier or civilian—had illusions left about any glamor or adventure in warfare. War was something to be forgotten—if it could be forgotten.

CHAPTER 15

Soldiers Are Still with Us

Historians of the future will probably lump the two world wars together, as they have lumped together the Punic Wars and the Peloponnesian Wars. Who now, except historians, knows that there were three great wars between Rome and Carthage, with intervals of twenty-three and fifty-two years between them?

Only twenty years passed between the close of World War I and the beginning of World War II. Hopeful people labeled the first of those terrible conflicts "the war to end wars." Less hopeful people weren't so sure. Hardly had the armistice been signed than trouble broke out again—war between Greece and Turkey; a bloody, merciless civil war in Russia; other disturbances the world over.

Even hopeful people began to realize that "the war to end wars" had ended nothing and solved nothing. The decades of the 20's and 30's were uneasy years. Echoes of 1914-18 still sounded through the feverish 20's and the depression-ridden 30's. It became apparent to men with foresight—Winston Churchill of Britain among them—that a new and more terrible war was shaping up. Italy had fallen into the hands of a posturing rabble-rouser named Benito Mussolini, leader of the Fascist party, who preached the nobility of war and armed boys with miniature rifles to form his new "Roman legions." Germany, bitter and impoverished, came under the control of a rabble-rouser a thousand times more dangerous: Adolf Hitler, head of the National Socialist (Nazi) party. On the other side of the world, Japan, restless and ambitious, began to swallow chunks of China.

Hardly anyone listened to the warnings of leaders like Churchill. The World War had been over for years but people were still too weary of war, too worn out by what they had lived through. They preferred to believe there could never be another war, and they turned a deaf ear and a blind eye to what was going on in the world.

To try out his legions, Mussolini invaded the ancient African empire of Ethiopia. A devastating civil war broke out in Spain—a war used by Italy, Germany, and Soviet Russia to test their new weapons and military theories. Japan stepped up its invasion of China and began to talk about bringing all of East Asia under Japanese rule. Hitler annexed Austria, a remnant of the once-proud empire, and carved up Czechoslovakia. And still hopeful people talked of "peace in our time" and found eager listeners.

In 1939 Hitler signed a treaty with Russia. Neither side had any intention of honoring the treaty a minute longer than it had to, but for the moment it gave Hitler a free hand. With Germany's eastern frontier safeguarded by the treaty, Hitler in 1939 invaded Poland. A few days later England and France entered the struggle and World War II had begun.

A generation has grown up since the atomic bombs at

Hiroshima and Nagasaki ended the war in 1945, but it is still too close, and altogether too vast, for us to see it truly in perspective. The war was fought on a scale that dwarfed even the conflagration of 1914.

War flamed the length and breadth of China. Battles raged in tropical Asia; in Scandinavia; in Italy; in the Balkan Mountains and in Africa. Soldiers fought and died in Egypt and on the island of Crete, sites of two of the earth's oldest civilizations. Soldiers fought equally hard, and died equally heroically, on remote Pacific islands whose people were still living in the Stone Age. Who now, except those who fought there, remembers the names of those islands—Kwajalein, Maloelap, Peleliu, Makin? Each had its day in the headlines, then receded again into obscurity.

Much of the war—as it had been twenty-five years earlier—was fought on the old, old battlegrounds of western Europe.

The Germans aimed their punch again at Paris, and this time the plan worked. They drove the British forces out of continental Europe and occupied Paris, something they had not succeeded in doing a quarter century earlier. Hitler broke his treaty with Russia and invaded the Soviet Union, driving deep into that vast country. The Germans occupied Greece and a great part of North Africa. Japan, meanwhile, swept through the Far East, occupied the rich Dutch East Indies, overthrew the great British base at Singapore, and threatened Australia. In the process the Japanese attacked the huge American naval base at Pearl Harbor, and brought the United States into the conflict. One by one, most of the nations of Europe, and indeed of the whole world, were drawn into the war. Only Spain, Sweden, and Switzerland, of the European countries, managed to stay neutral. It was truly a world at war.

But what of the soldiers?

There was a vast difference in the way the two world wars were fought. For the great majority of men who took part in it, the first war meant long, agonized months in the trenches: monotony, filth, and misery. Two veterans of that war could be fairly sure of finding a common ground of experience. One might have fought at Ypres, the other at the Somme; one might have gone home wounded in 1915, the other might not have been recruited until 1917. But each had fought the same kind of war in the same way; each knew what the other was talking about.

Not so for the soldiers of the second war. It was primarily a war of movement. Only in a few instances—the terrible sieges of Stalingrad and Leningrad, for example —did the fighting resemble the slugging matches of the Western Front in World War I. By 1940 offense had finally caught up with defense. The Second World War was largely a series of lightning moves, fast attacks, surprises, and maneuvers—the kind of tactics the Germans called *blitzkrieg*, or "lightning war." The change was due almost entirely to the great improvement in transport.

No longer did armies have to rely mainly on their own feet, plus thousands of pack animals and a comparatively few primitive trucks. The war was carried on with a bewildering variety of vehicles powered by gasoline or diesel engines. These included trucks of all sizes and shapes; the many-purpose "jeep"; light tanks, medium tanks, heavy tanks, tank destroyers; weapons carriers; self-propelled artillery; armored cars; amphibious craft;

ships and boats of strange design and specialized uses.

And most of all, airplanes. In place of the handful of wood-and-canvas "aeroplanes" of the first war were whole fleets of fast, maneuverable aircraft, much more durable and much more heavily armed. In the twenty years of shaky peace between the wars, the plane had been transformed from an interesting sideshow to one of the main weapons of war. Bombers and fighters, dive-bombers, cargo and troop carriers, scouts, weather planes, torpedo planes, artillery spotters, helicopters, planes adapted especially for night use, planes built for the use of parachute troops—all these and more added vastly to the speed and movement of the war.

Improvement in the technology of war greatly complicated the job of being a soldier. New kinds of transport, new weapons, and new scientific devices like radar meant that to a much greater degree than in any previous war a soldier had to be a specialist. Hundreds of thousands of soldiers rarely or never fired a gun. They were mechanics, or truck drivers, or construction engineers, or experts in loading ships, building airstrips, meteorology, dietetics. So many and so diverse were the jobs soldiers had to do that they made jokes about being in the "1451st Mess Kit Repair Unit" or said, "This guy says he's in the infantry. What's infantry?"

The vast size and scope of the war precluded, in a large measure, the close feelings that the soldiers of World War I had for one another. The Second World War actually was a dozen different wars, fought in different ways, all going on at the same time. What had a tank driver who fought in North Africa in common with a foot soldier who campaigned in the pestilential swamps of New Guinea? Or with the operator of a bulldozer in

the Aleutian Islands, or a paratrooper who landed in France? All were combat veterans of the army; but except for some experiences shared in basic training, perhaps, each would find it hard to understand what the others had gone through.

A veteran of both wars said that the soldier of 1942 was "infinitely better led, better fed, and better trained" than his father who fought in 1918. This is undoubtedly true. He was also far better cared for. Medical science had made tremendous advances between the wars—the sulfa drugs alone saved thousands of lives, administration of blood plasma thousands more. Many a man today owes his life to the speed with which he was taken from a fighting front, often by plane, to a hospital after he was wounded. A similar wound in the first war would probably have been fatal.

More attention was paid to the men's mental condition, too. What had been called "shell shock" was now "combat fatigue," recognized earlier and treated more effectively. The U.S. government and army administration made special efforts to maintain high morale. There were movies, recreation areas, touring entertainers, organized sports and games, and above all, prompt delivery of mail from home. So much attention was paid to morale, in fact, that there were charges that soldiers were being pampered and spoiled.

There was far less of a gulf between officers and enlisted men than there had been in earlier wars, even in such tradition-bound armies as the German and the British. One reason was that a far higher percentage of officers had come up through the ranks and knew what it was like to be a private. The gulf was still far from obliterated, though, and private soldiers were reminded of it every day. The old system under which officers were gentlemen, and enlisted men were not, still hung on. One American general drew down wrath on his head for following military etiquette and issuing invitations to a reception which read: "Officers and their ladies and enlisted men and their wives."

All in all, the soldier of World War II was far better off than the soldier of World War I—in equipment, in training, in care, in leadership. And above all, because he was spared the grisly horror of trench warfare.

But that does not mean that World War II was a sort of gigantic picnic. It was total war on a scale never dreamed of before—vicious, bitter, exhausting fighting which demanded at least as much stamina and courage as any war ever fought. For sheer scope of destruction and loss of life, World War II stands alone. The staggering total of 67,381,000 men were under arms in the combatant nations. And of that total, more than 16½ million died!

Civilians suffered far worse than in any previous war. Refugees from invaded areas died by the thousands, and air raids by both sides killed hundreds of thousands of women and children. No one has any accurate idea what the grand total of deaths directly attributable to the war may be.

It took five years, and an incalculable amount of blood and suffering, before World War II was ended. Italy was the first member of the "Axis" to give up. The Italians had never been enthusiastic about the war and had achieved no notable success in it; in 1943 they overthrew Mussolini, put him to death, and resigned from the fighting. Germany, beaten far worse than she had been in 1918, capitulated in 1945; Japan, facing obliteration by the atomic bomb, gave up a few months later. The end of hostilities, unfortunately, did not mean the end of problems for the world.

Each year since 1945 has seen some part of the world torn by war: Indo-China, Algeria, tropical Africa, India, the Near East. The war fought in Korea in 1950-53 between United Nations soldiers, mostly Americans and South Koreans, on the one hand and Communist North Koreans and Chinese on the other, was a major war, though it was tiny by comparison with the huge conflict which preceded it. Uncertainties, tension, and nervousness grip the world today, due largely to the aggressive policies of Communism, the breakup of the old colonial system, and the restlessness and instability of new nations. For this, in turn, the two world wars are largely to blame.

The hideous power of the atomic and hydrogen bombs makes it quite possible that another world war would mean the end of mankind, and almost certainly the end of civilization. That such a war will never come is the prayer of everyone.

In our troubled world, soldiers are still very much with us. We are used to them; they are a part of life. The sight of young men, and even young women, in uniform is so commonplace that we do not even give them a second glance. We do not look on soldiers with horror or contempt or fear, as other ages have done. Soldiers are relatives and friends, and probably at least one member of everyone's family has an old uniform put away somewhere, a souvenir of his days in the service.

Young men accept the idea that sooner or later they will have to put on a similar uniform and be soldiers themselves for a while. Not many are overjoyed at the prospect but not many are horrified at it, either. It is something that young men do. Boys still in grade school discuss what branch of the service they plan to join when they grow up—a subject of conversation that never would have crossed the minds of boys in the 1920's, or the 1900's, or the 1880's.

Military service is something that comes with being a man, just as it was in the days when the bronze age spearman marched off with the other men of his tribe. For most, it is not a special profession, or a service entered into by only one class of society. Neither is it a highly exalted, almost mystical kind of duty in which a soldier seeks personal honor and glory, as the knight did.

Most of our soldiers today would rather be something else. They are quite aware there is no glamor or romance in war. But they know, as well, that they are doing what must be done to serve the cause of peace and freedom —and they do it willingly.

For Further Reading

Vast quantities of material have been written on military history, on warfare, and on soldiers. This list contains only a few of the least technical and most useful books.

Adcock, F. E., *Greece and Macedonian Art of War*. Berkeley, Calif.: University of California Press, 1962.

Blakeslee, F. G., *Army Uniforms of the World*. Private printing, 1919.

Creasy, Sir Edward S., *15 Decisive Battles of the World*, revised edition. New York: Colonial Press, 1899.

Downey, Fairfax, *Sound of the Guns*. New York: David McKay Co., 1956.

Edwards, Maj. T. J., *Military Customs*. London: Gale & Polden, 1950.

Hewitt, John, *Ancient Armor and Weapons in Europe*. London, 1860.

Judy, William Lewis, *A Soldier's Diary*. Judy Publishing Co., 1930.

Ketchum, Richard M., *The Battle of Bunker Hill*. Garden City, N.Y.: Doubleday & Co., 1962.

Laver, James, *British Military Uniforms*. London, 1948.

Manucy, Albert, *Artillery Through the Ages*. Washington: U.S. Government Printing Office, 1955.

Martin, Joseph Plumb, *Private Yankee Doodle*, ed., George F. Scheer. Boston: Little, Brown & Co., 1962.

McCormick, Robert R., *The Army of 1918*. New York: Harcourt, Brace, 1920.

Miraux, Emile, *Daily Life in the Time of Homer*. New York: Macmillan Co., 1959.

Mitchell, Col. William A., *Outlines of World Military History*. Harrisburg, Pa.: Military Service Publishing Co., 1935.

Ogden, Henry A., *A Boy's Book of Famous Regiments*. New York: R. M. McBride Co., 1929.

Preston, Richard A., Wise, Sydney F., Werner, Herman O., and Praeger, Frederick A., *Men in Arms; A history of warfare and its interrelationships with Western society*. New York: Praeger Publishing Co., 1956.

Ridgeway, Sir William, *The Early Age of Greece*. New York: Cambridge University Press, 1931.

Scheer, George F., and Rankin, Hugh F., *Rebels and Redcoats*. New York: World Publishing Co., 1957.

Spaulding, Col. Oliver L., *A Study of Military Methods from Earliest Times*. Washington: Infantry Journal Press, 1957.

Stallings, Laurence, *The Doughboys*. New York: Harper & Row, 1963.

Stern, Philip Van Doren, *Soldier Life in Union and Confederate Armies*. Greenwich, Conn.: Fawcett Publishing Co., 1961.

Symons, Arthur, *Soldiers and What They Do*. New York: F. Watts, 1958.

Todd, Frederick P., *Soldiers of the American Army*. Chicago: Henry Regnery Co., 1954.

Toynbee, Arnold, *War and Civilization,* selections from *A Study of History.* New York: Oxford University Press, 1950.

Tunis, Edwin, *Weapons.* Cleveland: World Publishing Co., 1954.

Watteville, Col. H., *The British Soldier.* New York: G. P. Putnam's Sons, 1961.

Wintringham, Thomas H., *Story of Weapons and Tactics; from Troy to Stalingrad.* Boston: Houghton Mifflin, 1943.

Wolff, Leon, *In Flanders Fields.* New York: Viking Press, 1958.

Index

220